You Can't Make It Up!

By
Nell Bridge Cahn

Copyright

Dedication

I want to dedicate this book to my exceptional family.

A special thanks to my daughter, Susan Cahn Abelman; my daughter-in-law, Marylyn Hawes Cahn; and Wanda Simpson. Without their help, there would be no book.

Table of Contents

Introduction

My family came to the United States from Kyiv, Russia, in the early 1900s and settled in Monroe, Louisiana. My Uncle Joe Kusin and Aunt Dena Kaplan Kusin were the first to arrive. My grandparents, Max Kaplan and Bessie Hoffman Kaplan, followed several years later with their children: Rose, David, and Ethel. My mother, Sara Freida Kaplan, was born a year after they arrived on February 21, 1913. It was never clear how the family ended up in Monroe.

Grandma Bessie Kaplan.

Upon arriving, Uncle Joe started a pushcart business. It only took him a short time to figure out what would sell. Pillows were in great demand. So, each night after dinner, Uncle Joe and Aunt Dena would spend their evenings making pillows to sell on the cart the next day. He managed to save enough money to rent a small building, and along with the pillows, he began to manufacture mattresses. Uncle Joe named the company "Dixie Bedding." Years later, as the business grew, he changed the name to "Dixie Bedding and Furniture."

By 1912, it became clear that if my grandparents, Max and Bessie Kaplan, and their children were going to leave Russia for the United States, they had to do it immediately. If they had delayed, it would have been impossible to get out. When I was very young, I recall Grandpa Max sitting on the couch reading his newspaper, which was written in Yiddish[1]. I remember him saying, "Little Nell, I marched in the Russian army for 3 cents a day."

By the time Grandpa Max and his family arrived in Monroe, Uncle Joe was doing so well with the mattress factory that he turned over the pushcart business to my grandpa. The pushcart business continued to be very lucrative as Monroe was beginning to grow. grandpa recognized that there was a growing demand for large pieces of metal used in construction. He began buying small pieces of property along the railroad track to store all the things that were too large for the cart. One year later, Grandpa Max and Uncle David started their business on the corner of 9th and Adams Street and named it "M. Kaplan and Son." The family home was on Washington Street, just two blocks away from the business.

Grandpa always advised, "You should buy commercial property on the railroad track and residential property on the water." He also said that it wasn't what was on top of the ground that mattered; it was what was under the ground that made money.

Grandpa had an innate sixth sense for business, and not only was the scrap business booming, but so was oil. Everyone was speculating. People wanting to drill would come to Grandpa Max and Uncle David with a desire to trade pipe and equipment for an interest in their well.

---

[1] **Yiddish** is the language of the Ashkenazim, central and eastern European Jews and their descendants. Written in the Hebrew alphabet, it became one of the world's most widespread languages, appearing in most countries with a Jewish population by the 19th century.

Uncle David and grandpa thought letting drillers have their pipe for an interest in their well was a "good" way to go broke. They would allow cash and carry only.

My mother and her sister Ethel ("Ecca") graduated from Monroe City High School and then went off to finishing school[2] at the prestigious Ward-Belmont in Nashville, Tennessee. When Mother and Ecca returned from Ward-Belmont, the city of Monroe had begun to grow and spread out. Folks were moving away from the center of town. Mother and Ecca convinced Grandpa Max that they needed a new classy house on the bayou. The depression was on the horizon, and money was tight. Since Grandpa had done business for cash, he was in an excellent position to take advantage of the situation and make a great investment. Cash was king!

---

[2] A finishing school is an educational institution that emphasizes cultural studies and social graces, preparing young women for adulthood and society.

A beautiful home at 1902 Island Drive went up for sale at a wonderful price. Somehow, my mother and Aunt Ecca convinced Grandpa that buying the house was the right thing to do.

Grandpa Max, Grandmother Bessie, Aunt Ecca, and my mother all moved from Washington Street to 1902 Island drive. After moving into their little palace, they hired a classy decorator from Shreveport, Louisiana. Mr. Westerdal came to Monroe to help decorate their new home. Today, great-grandson Tab Cahn and his wife, Marylyn Hawes Cahn, have the beautiful mahogany dining room set purchased from Friend Piper in Shreveport.

After finishing school, my mother attended Louisiana State University (LSU) for several years. The summer of her junior year, there was a big tennis tournament in Monroe. At the social, the evening before the tournament started, my Uncle David Kaplan and his Cousin Louis Kusin introduced an acquaintance of theirs, Maurice Bridge from Ardmore, Oklahoma, to my mother. The rest is history. Mother and Maurice married shortly thereafter. Aunt Clara and Uncle David held the wedding in their backyard on North 3rd Street and Auburn.

Grandpa Kaplan, Grandma Bessie Kaplan, Aunt Clara, and Uncle David Kaplan gave the couple enough money to return to Ardmore and rent an apartment for several months until Maurice could get his business going.

Uncle David Kaplan, Susan, Pawpaw, Nell, Freida, and Aunt Ecca.

Memories of Days Gone By

When my mother left my father in Ardmore, Oklahoma, and returned home to Monroe, she was three months pregnant with me.

I was born on August 12, 1935, at the Wright Bendel Clinic. My mother named me Nell, and I'm not sure for whom; I had no middle name because my mother could not think of one. Because of the Great Depression, money was tight, so my mother and I lived with my grandparents and my Aunt Ethel, whom we fondly called Ecca. Life, as we knew it, was good.

In 1940, faced with the threat of war, Grandpa decided the purchase of a new car was imminent. He arrived home the next evening with a beautiful black four-door Buick sedan. I would be starting the 1st grade at Georgia Tucker School, and he wanted to make sure I had transportation. I was in 2nd grade when Pearl Harbor was attacked on December 7, 1941. America was officially at war, and our lives changed forever.

A year later, my mother was driving our Buick, and my cousin Joel Sugar and I were in the back seat. We were broadsided by someone who ran a stop sign. The car flipped over and ended upside down on top of a fireplug that went through the roof. The firemen cut the doors open with an ax. It was an act of God—a miracle—that we were alive and unhurt. There were no cars available to buy, and we had no transportation.

Grandpa and Uncle David were in what they called the "Steel Fabrication Business." It seems to me now that it was more like the scrap business. Somehow, Grandpa managed to get a 1934 two-door Buick Coupe. The car looked more like a rusty old tin can with no tires. In 1942, due to the shortage of rubber, no tires were being manufactured for public consumption. Grandpa and Uncle David were doing business at Selman Field, the air force base in Monroe. They were able to commandeer four airplane tires for the car. We had wheels, but how humiliating for a youngster of eight, almost nine years old, being driven to school in this awful rusty tin can mounted on four monster tires.

Aunt Clara, my Uncle David's wife, felt sorry for me because I was so embarrassed about the car. The situation was beginning to affect my grades. My cousin Charleen was four years older than me, but we were both enrolled at Georgia Tucker. Aunt Clara told my mother to drop me off at their house before 8:00 A.M., and it would be no problem for me to ride when their chauffeur, Ladell, took Charleen to school in the morning and picked her up in the afternoon. Once again, life was good, and I did not have to be seen riding around in the awful car… or so I thought!

A few months went by, and I desperately needed a new pair of shoes. I had begun to grow, and my old ones didn't fit anymore. Mother told me that on the upcoming Saturday morning, she would take me to the Family Shoe Store on Desiard, the main street of town. We would be there at the stroke of 10:00 AM when the store opened. I still remember her saying that we would purchase the shoes and be home before I knew it, and no one would see me in the car.

Saturday came, and off we went to buy shoes. Unfortunately, my mother, God bless her, forgot the circus was in town. There was a traffic jam on Desiard, and the circus parade was on our heels when our car stopped running. The marching band was behind us. There was a trapeze artist on an elephant, cages of lions and tigers pulled by horses, and clowns dancing down the street. A policeman walked up

2

to the car and said, "Listen, lady, you have to get this pile of junk out of the way." I still remember hearing my mother saying, "I can't." He then wanted to know what the problem was. My mother said, "Sir, I can't find the accelerator." The policeman said, "Where do you think it went?" She looked him straight in the eyes and said, "Well, I think it's gone through the rusty old floorboard."

At this point, the policeman left, shaking his head, and returned with three clowns from the circus parade. They scratched their heads for a few minutes, and with us still in the car, they began to move us down the main street. They pushed us several blocks into a parking lot where a bunch of spectators were trying to watch the parade. The clowns walked away without a word. Lucky for us, our neighbors were on the corner watching the parade and gave us a ride home. Grandpa had the car towed later that day, but unfortunately, a few days later, it was back on Island Drive in the garage. Life does have its embarrassing moments. Monday morning at school, several of my friends who had attended the parade were duly impressed and wanted to know how the heck I was able to ride in the circus parade.

Well, there is justice; several months go by, and one day, my mother was late returning home from her bridge game and was in a rush to get ready for her date. Mother was a frequent smoker and was often seen with one in her hand. She put the little car in the garage and thought she snuffed out her cigarette in the ashtray. She closed the garage door and went to the house to change clothes. Her date Bernie who would soon become my new stepfather. I went to sleep and woke a short time later to the sound of sirens and a sky that was "very orange." I jumped out of bed and finally found my grandparents and Aunt Ecca on the back porch, watching the garage with the car burn to a crisp... it was probably the happiest day of my life.

There was not much excitement on a Saturday evening in Monroe, Louisiana, so everyone followed the fire trucks. Most of the town was watching the old car and garage burn to the ground when my mother and future stepdad drove up. I ran up to the window of their car, and I still remember my mother saying, "My goodness, we've been all over town looking for excitement. No wonder we couldn't find anyone; they're all right here watching the fire."

Fond Memories of Island Drive

My mother, an avid bridge player, was always hosting a bridge game. One day, she told me that my duty was to welcome the ladies when they arrived. Since my maiden name was Bridge, and my mother was always saying she was having a bridge game, I think I was a little confused. I stood at the front door and said, "Hi, my name is Nell Bridge Game, and my mother is serving chocolate pie for dessert." Ugh!

Ethel Masur was one of the regulars in my mother's bridge game. She and her husband were living with her husband's parents until their house was finished. Her father-in-law, Sig Masur, who owned "The Palace," a very fine department store, had just purchased a new LaSalle car. Sig was leaving on a buying trip to New York and had told the chauffeur that no one was allowed to drive the car. Miss Ethel, as we called her, was very beautiful. She had a cunning way with the men, so somehow, she convinced the chauffeur that it would be perfectly OK if she drove the LaSalle to the bridge game. Miss Ethel picked up all the ladies, pulled the car into the driveway at the house, and parked it. They were on the sun porch playing away when they heard horns honking. There was conversation as to what was going on outside. One of the women looked out the window and said she thought someone was pulling into the driveway; another of the ladies thought someone was backing out. The noise settled down, and they went back to their game. When the game was finished, one of the ladies walked out the front door as Miss Ethel said, "Where is the car?" It was nowhere in sight. I remember running across the street, down the bayou bank, and yelling, "It is over here." The car had rolled into the bayou. Nothing was visible except the headlights. Miss Ethel was hysterical, and rightfully so. The wrecker came and towed the car to the dealership. Miss Ethel begged and pleaded with them to have the car fixed by the time Sig returned from New York and requested not to say a word.

Well, believe it or not, the LaSalle was back by the time Sig returned, and all seemed to be well. No one had said a word. About a week went by, and Miss Ethel thought she had "dodged the bullet." The car was running fine and did not smell of fish. Mr. Sig was none the wiser until he went to the Petroleum Club for lunch, and someone came up and slapped him on the back and said, "Sig, how is your car running since it rolled into the bayou at the Kaplan's house?" Miss Ethel's marriage was over shortly after that, and she returned to Tuscaloosa, Alabama, with her two young children: her son Charles Masur and daughter Sylvia.

Another vivid memory of mine is that my mother absolutely adored hot tamales. There was a man who had a hot tamale cart at Five Points in Monroe. Five Points was not the greatest neighborhood for a young lady to be going to by herself, but Mother didn't care. She would go buy the hot tamales, bring them home, and "pig out." Grandpa, who spoke English poorly and could not pronounce my mother's name correctly—her name was Freida—called her Fedie. Grandpa said, "Fedie, there is something bad wrong with those tamales; you should not be eating them." My mother did not care, and every Saturday, she would go to get her hot tamale fix. One Sunday morning, my mother sat down at the breakfast table and picked up the newspaper. She looked at the front page and let out this awful scream. The headlines read, "*HOT TAMALE MAN Arrested for Making Tamales out of Cats.*" There was a photograph of his backyard with hundreds of catheads—so much for hot tamales. My mother swore until her dying day that, given half a chance, she would eat them all over again.

World War II was heating up, and the US Air Force Base at Selman Field was in full swing. It was a training base for fighter pilots. The Rabbi put out a notice to the congregants urging them to be gracious and open their homes to as many soldiers as they could for Friday night dinner. There were several who came to our house regularly. We never knew who was coming to dinner; we only knew how many were coming. It was sad when one of the regulars did not show because we knew he had to ship out. Friday nights were always fun and upbeat. The men were so happy to be away from the base, and the dinner was always extra special. Aunt Ecca played the piano, and we would all gather around and sing. Some of our favorite songs were *"Pack Up Your Troubles," "When Johnny Comes Marching Home,"* and all the WWII oldies. The old house rocked.

Our Pet Family

My first experience of puppy love was a beautiful white Spitz we named Prince. Prince only left my side when it was time for my nap, and then he was banished to the outside. Summers were very hot in Monroe, so Prince would find refuge under the car that was usually parked in the driveway. One day, my mother forgot to check under the car before backing out, and you can imagine the rest of the story. Mother explained to me that Prince had become an Angel. He had been called back to heaven to take care of little girls like me who did not have anyone to take care of them. We had a beautiful funeral for Prince under the Weeping Willow tree in the backyard.

Several years passed, and I really missed not having a dog. My grandparents surprised me on my ninth birthday with an adorable black Cocker Spaniel they named Buna.

Buna was named after the synthetic rubber that was manufactured in occupied Poland using slave labor from among prisoners of Auschwitz and raw materials from the formerly Polish coalfields. She was my love and my best friend. Buna passed away soon after I finished my first year at Stephens College.

My mother decided that since I would be returning to college in the fall, another dog was probably not a good idea. One day, unbeknown to my stepdad and me, my mother arrived home with a cage and a little blue parakeet named Caruso.

Caruso was a character that entertained us all. The bird was trained to come out of the cage and return on command. Caruso loved to fly to the mantle, dance up and down, and chatter away. In the summer, we use the attic fan to keep the air circulating. The return air had a very strong suction. One day, Caruso decided to fly around the room instead of going directly to the mantle. Unfortunately, it was a day the attic fan was running. As you can imagine, that was a very sad day for all of us.

From that point on, my mother was pretty much finished having any pets.

Abry and I had not been married very long when he arrived home one day with a straggly-looking white terrier with a big brown spot over one eye. Abry had found him in the back alley of Cahn Electric on Milam Street as he was getting in his car to come home one evening. We named him Buster Brown.

Buster Brown was nothing like my previous dogs, who were wonderful. He was hyper and untrainable. Buster Brown destroyed everything that wasn't nailed down; he made our lives miserable.

When we left the house, we would close Buster Brown up in the kitchen because we felt there was nothing he could destroy. One evening, upon returning from dinner, we entered the house through the kitchen door. There was something all over the floor. I asked Abry, "What in the world is that all over the floor?" Abry said, "Look at your kitchen cabinets." The dog had chewed half of the doors off all the bottom cabinets. We knew it was time for Buster Brown to go because we had both had it. Abry found Buster Brown a nice home with one of the electricians who worked for us. When they came to pick him up, I think the only feeling we had was a feeling of relief. I am happy Buster Brown had a happy home and a very good life with them.

Susan Yum Yum, Tab, and Nell.

Several years passed, and we were busy raising the children and had our hands full. When Tab started school, and he and Susan were no longer at home, I found the house was very empty, and I was lonesome. I started thinking how nice it would be to have a little dog. One day, I saw a "For Sale" ad in the paper for a female little black poodle puppy. My thinking was that it wouldn't hurt just to go and look. I was hooked, and there was no way I wasn't going to have that dog. I rounded up Abry, Susan, and Tab, and off we went to check out the puppy. It was sort of dirty pool on my part because I knew Abry would have a hard time saying "no" to the kids. Abry tried to say "no" but finally gave in. We had a new member of the family, and we named her Yum Yum.

Susan was Yum Yum's favorite, and she would not leave her side. She slept under Susan's bed, and it became impossible to get her out even to eat. One night, Abry tied a piece of meat on the end of a string and tied the other end to the doorknob on Susan's bedroom door. When Yum Yum came out to eat the meat, Abry slammed the door behind her. We finally had to start keeping the dog in a kennel in the kitchen. Yum Yum did not like that very much; she became an escape artist. She figured out how to flip open the latch with her nose and escape the cage. We finally had to tie a little rope around the latch.

Susan and Yum Yum.

An acquaintance of mine had a male black poodle, and for some reason, she convinced me that if Yum Yum had a litter, it might make her feel better. I thought that was a good idea because I thought my mother really needed a dog. The lady told me that poodles usually had three dogs in a litter. She would take the first pick. I could sell one to cover the cost, and there would be one for my mother. Abry was opposed to this plan, but the more I thought about it, the better I liked the idea.

We mated the dogs, and Yum Yum was expecting. She had a very difficult labor, and we ended up taking her to the vet to have the puppies delivered. Everything went almost as we had planned. Yum Yum had three puppies. There was only one problem—only one puppy survived. I was crying when Abry came home. When I told him what had happened, he looked at me and said, "Well honey, looks like you have a problem unless the lady picks one of the dead ones." We all knew that wasn't going to happen.

The one little puppy was a little girl and just adorable. She was like a little wind-up toy. The kids named her Little Yum. Yum Yum and Little Yum were so happy together. It was just what Yum Yum needed. Unfortunately, the day of reckoning arrived, and the lady called to tell me she would pick up Little Yum on Friday. It was a sad day for the Cahns. We all stood in the kitchen and cried when Little Yum left.

Yum Yum became impossible when she realized Little Yum was gone for good. Yum Yum was mad at everyone. We couldn't have her around the kids. I didn't know what I was going to do when I had a phone call from the lady who had Little Yum. She said that because Little Yum was not a show-quality dog, she couldn't afford to keep her. It was simply too expensive. She would be bringing her back that afternoon. We were all ecstatic; Little Yum was coming home.

Unfortunately, that happiness was short-lived because Abry said he was not having two dogs in the house. We had to choose. Abry was not to be reasoned with. I knew we could not separate the dogs again and couldn't make a choice. My friend Martha Ghio, who had loved both little dogs, offered to take them both, and as hard as it was, we all realized that was the best possible solution. Martha, wherever you are, you deserve a place in heaven.

It wasn't too long after Yum and Little Yum were gone that Abry was offered a German Shepherd puppy by a friend whose dog had a very large litter. There was a dog in the litter that Abry fell in love with and agreed to take. We named him Poker, and until the day he died, he was Abry's best friend. They went to obedience school, and Abry trained him every morning and every evening. They were inseparable. Poker loved everyone and was a great friend to Susan and Tab.

I think Abry always felt a little guilty about not letting us keep Yum and Little Yum. When Susan came home one day and said her friend knew of an apricot poodle puppy in need of a home and she would love to have her for her birthday present, Abry agreed. Susan named her Ginger.

Above: Poker and Tab.

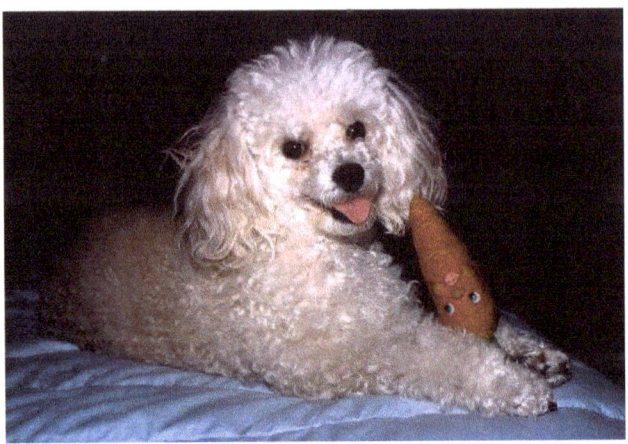

Below: Ginger

13

Ginger was three years younger than Poker, and they became best friends. Of course, Ginger was an inside dog, and Poker was an outside dog, but they loved each other and played together constantly. When Poker died at a ripe old age, it wasn't very long after that Ginger passed away. We always felt that she died of a broken heart.

Susan and Ginger.

It was the year 2000 before another puppy found its way into our hearts. My friend Jean Brown called one day and invited me over because she had something very special to share. When I walked into the room, everyone was sitting in a circle on the floor with three of the cutest Shih Tzu puppies I had ever seen. Before I could say anything, one of the puppies removed himself from the circle and ran right over to me. Guess what? He needed a home, and I knew I had the perfect one for him. I wrote Jean's granddaughter a check for $200.00, headed for the vet to check the dog out, and then quickly stopped at the pet store for supplies.

Tab and Ginger.

When I arrived home with the dog and all the supplies, Abry was furious. He wanted to know why I had not asked his permission. I told him I didn't ask because I knew he would say "no." He wanted to know how long I had been planning this. I told him it was "totally unplanned parenthood." Abry told me not to expect him to have anything to do with the dog. I said, "That's fine with me." I named my little dog Button because the minute I saw him, I thought his little round face looked just like a button.

Abry was not very nice to Button, and the little dog didn't understand why. It was sad for me to watch. Button was determined to win him over, which he finally did. However, it took Button about two years. Button would sit by Abry's chair, looking for some acknowledgment that he was there. If Abry would lie down in bed to watch TV, Button would go and sit by his bed. Button made it impossible for Abry to ignore him. It was such a happy day when I walked into the kitchen one morning and caught Abry talking baby talk to Button.

During the fall of 2003, I had a very bad allergy attack, and Abry volunteered to take over the responsibility of walking the dog. It had been a long time since Poker had died, and I think Abry really enjoyed the chore of his morning walk with Button. When I recovered from the allergy and felt okay, I decided to join them on the walk. I was delighted when I heard Abry start to chant a little poem that Button seemed to enjoy walking to. Button's Chant went something like this:

One, Two, Three, Four

I know what you are walking for.

Two, Four, Six, Eight

Poop out all the food you ate.

Six, Five, Four, Three

Lift your leg and make a Pee.

Sound off

One, Two, Three, Four

Abry and Button.

It was almost as if Button would pee on command. After Button watered the fireplug and several bushes, Pops said, "Button, I'm going to take you to Carnegie Hall because you are the pianist dog I ever saw.

It broke my heart in July of 2016 when we lost Button. I swore that I never again would have another dog; losing him was just too painful. To this day, I still tear up when I think about my precious angel.

So here we are today, March 27, 2020, and I am sitting at my computer reliving happy and sad memories of all the furry friends that I have loved and lost. I am so grateful for my wonderful memories. As I look over at my precious apricot poodle, Sissy, who has kept me company for two years and is sleeping peacefully in her little bed without a care in the world, I feel that we are so lucky to have each other. We have been quarantined for two weeks now with the threat of the coronavirus, and I have no idea what tomorrow will bring. Today, we are, well, happy and enjoying the moment.

Susan, Marilyn, Button, Tab, Chandler, and Nell.

Aunt Clara & Uncle David

A unt Clara and Uncle David had a great influence on helping me have a life as normal as possible. Uncle David was the father I did not have in those early years, and Aunt Clara, who was the caretaker personified, saw to it that I was included in as many of their family activities as possible. In the summertime, when it cooled off in the evenings, Aunt Clara, Uncle David, and their two daughters, Charlene and Shirley, would drive over to the house and pick me up. One of the special treats was stopping at the Watermelon Garden for a piece of ice-cold watermelon. I was usually sound asleep in somebody's lap by the time we returned home. Thinking back, it was all the little things that made my life so wonderful.

Aunt Clara came from a very wealthy family in Bastrop, Louisiana. For some unknown reason, possibly health, she had no schooling past the fourth grade. However, she had an unbelievable appreciation for beauty and fine things. She was a collector of antiques and works of art. Among some of her prized possessions were the first editions of all the J.J.Audubon's books. Unfortunately, she was not proficient in the English grammar. I remember, on numerous occasions, my mother saying, poor Aunt Clara just massacres the English language. One of Aunt Clara's many favorite possessions was a magnificent sterling silver epergne that graced her dining room table, which she called her "Apron." My mother would cringe when she heard her say that, especially to someone who was socially prominent. It didn't matter to me what Aunt Clara said; I loved her anyway. She called me baby, and that always made me feel loved and cared for. Aunt Clara had a couple of sayings; one of my favorites was, "When in Rome shoot a Roman Candle," and the other, "Where there is smoke, there is smoking." Her sayings have stayed with me my entire life, and I always smile when I think about her saying them.

Aunt Clara was a marvelous cook, and she loved to entertain. One of her dessert specialties was Coconut Cake. Even during the war, when certain food items were rationed, she always managed to serve lavish meals. One evening, she was entertaining some of the top brass stationed at Selman Field, the air force base in Monroe. For dessert, she made a huge coconut cake that must have been three layers tall. When the maid brought the cake to the table, I think everyone's mouth fell open. One of the officers said, "Oh, Mrs. Kaplan, that cake is magnificent. I must ask you, though, how in the world were you able to swing this with the ration of sugar?" My Aunt, may God rest her soul, replied without missing a beat. She said, "I knew rationing was coming, so for two years, I have been whoring sugar in my attic."

Aunt Clara ran the house like it was a hotel. She required sheets to be changed every day. I remember the back porch was set up like a laundry. She had a huge roller where the laundress would press the sheets through the rollers. It was quite a production. Mamie, who was their housekeeper, would sit on the porch and supervise. I still remember her sitting in the old rocking chair, sewing away. Mamie did beautiful embroidery. She handmade our nightgowns, camisoles, and petticoats. She trimmed them with little pink roses and blue satin ribbon. Mine never had quite as much lace and ribbons as Charlene and Shirley's, but they were beautiful, and I was so proud of them.

I experienced my first trip with the family in the summer when I was ten years old. There was no longer a ration of gasoline, and life, as we knew it, was good.

With Uncle David at the wheel of the old green Studebaker, Aunt Clare, Charlene, Shirley, my mother, and I headed for the Ozarks[3]. I have no idea how we all fit in the car, but I don't remember anyone complaining. We stayed at a resort on the lake in Eureka Springs, Arkansas. We swam in the beautiful lake, hiked the mountain trails, and had a glorious week. At night, after dinner, a bingo game was held in the lodge. The cost was ten cents a game. It was there that I won my first Bingo game. The prize was $1.25, and with that came the pleasure of helping sweep up the floor in the lodge. On the way back to Monroe, we spent the weekend in Hot Springs at the Arlington Hotel. The hotel was so elegant that I thought I was living in a dream world.

---

[3] Spanning an area of more than 45,000 square land miles (roughly the size of the state of New York), the Ozarks covers most of the southern half of Missouri and northwestern and north central Arkansas, as well as much smaller portions of northeastern Oklahoma and southeastern Kansas.

New Family in Town

It was late August of 1938, and I had just turned three years old. I remember as plainly as the nose on my face the day my mother came into my room and said, "A new family has moved to town from Shreveport, and they have a little girl just your age. Her name is Minette. This afternoon, we are going to their house so you can meet her." My mother said to Ora, my nanny, "Please see to it that Nell is dressed and ready to go to visit Minette after her nap around 2:30." I recall being excited because it was lonesome being an only child and having no one to play with.

I was dressed to the nines in my little white pinafore with a big blue bow ribbon and little white baby doll shoes. I remember feeling very special. My mother always had a way of making me feel that I was the most beautiful person in the entire world.

Minette, and her Mother Minna greeted us at the door. Minette was the tiniest little thing I had ever seen. That day, I met my best friend for life. She became the person who knew me better than I knew myself. We did almost everything kids were supposed to do. We played dolls and paper dolls; we mastered the game of jacks and pick-up sticks on summer days when it was too hot to play outside.

One of our biggest pleasures was stealing the eggs and sugar from the kitchen and going outside to make mud pies. It was during wartime, and sugar was scarce. Eggs were a different story, we raised chickens in the back yard and eggs were always plentiful. We made little pies out of the mud, sugar, and eggs, and we lined them up in the driveway to cook. When my mother found out what we were doing, she was furious. I still remember her marching out the back door to the Weeping Willow tree, breaking off a branch, and I knew the handwriting was on the wall[4]. I was about to experience my first whipping. My mother made it very clear that if we ever tried that again, it would be my last time playing with Minette.

Minette and I started nursery school together and then on to the first grade at Georgia Tucker School. We were bonded for life to the friends we made that first year at Georgia Tucker.

There was an announcement in class one day that there would be a meeting for anyone who wanted to join the Brownie Scouts. Bettie Davis, the mother of our friend, Linda Davis, would be the Scout leader of the group. Eleven of us joined and went on from Brownie Scout to Girl Scout. We learned what it meant to support and care about other people. We learned kindness and charity, went camping, and learned to survive outdoors. We took classes in basket weaving and cooking.

Minette and I were still playing dolls when I met Abry, and we were dating. We were fourteen years old when Minette asked me, "What do you think Abry would say if he knew you and I are still playing dolls?" I think we both grew up that day. When Minette left the house, it was with great sadness because we both knew it was the last time to play with our dolls.

---

[4] The phrase "the handwriting on the wall" refers to a clear and obvious sign that something bad or negative is going to happen soon. It originates from the biblical story in the Book of Daniel, where mysterious writing appears on the wall during King Belshazzar's feast, predicting the fall of his kingdom.

Gifting

I remember my mother saying that a gift was not a gift unless it was something you wanted for yourself and that it was much better to give than to receive. She taught me the importance of giving and that selecting the perfect present for someone you loved was very important. I found out very early in our marriage that not everyone was raised with the same set of values.

Abry's first birthday present to me was the ugliest black satin envelope purse I had ever seen. Worse than that, after I explored the inside of the purse, I found a little white gift card that read, "To Jan," Abry's Mother, "Love from Wheetie," Abry's maternal grandmother. I was too hurt to confront him. As a matter of fact, until this day, I have never been able to tell anyone about the incident.

My first Christmas present from Abry was a pink bathrobe. It was the same thing my parents gave me, except it was not as pretty.

My friend Harriette and I loved to have lunch at a restaurant, "Dehans," on Milam Street. After lunch, we would walk over to Flournoy's and look at all the beautiful jewelry and dream. One of our outings was only a few weeks before Valentine's Day. At dinner that evening, Abry wanted to know about my day, and I told him about lunch and all the beautiful things we had seen at the jewelry store. There was one bracelet I loved, so I dropped what I thought was a subtle hint. Valentine's morning bright and early, Abry bopped into the bedroom with a small oblong box, just the shape of a bracelet. The box was beautifully wrapped with a red satin bow. I tore into the wrapping and printed on the lid of the box was "Peacocks," this was another jewelry store in Shreveport at the time. I was a little disappointed it wasn't from Flournoy's, but there was still hope. Until I opened the lid, and four stainless steel ice teaspoons fell onto my pregnant lap. I started to cry; Abry was completely baffled by my lack of appreciation for his gift. After all, he said, "Valentine isn't a major holiday, and we needed the four spoons to complete our set." He just didn't get it.

One Christmas, I remember clearly a beautifully wrapped box from the Fashion. In the '60s, the Fashion was a very elegant ladies' ready-to-wear store in Shreveport. I couldn't wait to open my present. When it was finally my turn, there, to my horror, was a gold knit dress and jacket identical to one I already had. The exception was that my mother had given me the dress as a gift when I visited them in New Orleans. My dress was very expensive; it was made of St. John knit from Saks. The dress Abry had given me was a copy, and he was so proud of his gift to me. He said he had seen the dress on someone and thought it was so beautiful that he thought it was the perfect gift. Somehow, I managed an exuberant "Thank you, honey." After Christmas, I took the dress back to the Fashion and exchanged it for something else. I wore the dress my mother had given me, and Abry never knew the difference.

What Abry lacked in the art of selecting presents, he made up for with the poems he wrote and clever cards. Hindsight, I wish I had saved all the precious cards and poems. The following is one that I really didn't care to remember.

Abry was quite the practical joker, and he was relentless. How he could come up with all this, I will never understand. It was probably around our third anniversary when I opened the present from my parents, and there were two blue Cloisonne Ming jars in the box. I found the anniversary card tucked in one of the jars that read, "Ashes to ashes, dust to dust, I hope to heavens Abry goes first." Happy

Anniversary, Mom and Dad. Of course, everyone at the party had a good idea of the culprit. I have no recollection of anyone holding their sides with laughter. I, for one, was in total shock.

The War is Over 1945

My Romance With The Game Of Bridge Began!

As World War II ended, there was another very serious war beginning, the war against Polio or Poliomyelitis, a crippling and potentially deadly infectious disease. Polio outbreaks in the United States were increasing in size, and several cases of the disease were prevalent in Monroe, Louisiana. Sadly, several children of friends of my parents died. It was a frightening time. When school was over for summer vacation, most of my friends were headed to summer camp in Wisconsin. My friend Shirley McDonald and I would be staying home. Our parents decided that the safest place for us was to remain in Monroe.

The public swimming pool was taboo as the Monroe Health Department put out a warning that it was better to stay out of crowds and away from public facilities. Picture shows were out of the question, but I learned something wonderful that summer. I learned how to entertain myself. I learned to love to read, and it is something I have enjoyed my entire life. Sally Archibald, our neighbor across the street, was an art teacher. Sally told my mother and me that I was welcome to come and paint any time. She had a little table set up in the corner of her studio, especially for me. I spent many happy mornings sitting in the corner at that little round table painting at Sally's.

Most afternoons, my friend Shirley McDonald would come to my house, or I would go over to her house – neither of which had air conditioning. We would lie across the bed and let the fans blow the awful hot air across us, trying to stay as cool as possible. Looking for a way to pass the time, I asked my mother to teach us how to play bridge, and that was the beginning of my lifelong fascination with the game.

Playing bridge was all we wanted to do from then on. I loved the game from the start. On nights I had no homework, I would beg my mother to invite her friends over so we could play. Shirk and Junie, two of my mother's friends, were delightful, formidable players who were always ready to accommodate us. I think they were fascinated by the fact that I was so young and taken with the game. On Saturday afternoons, when our friends were either playing golf or tennis, Shirley and I were at the Bayou Desiard Country Club playing duplicate bridge. Perhaps it is prophetic, or maybe it is just coincidental that my maiden name is Bridge.

MiMi

Mimi, as the children would call my mother, was her own person, and there was never anyone else like her. She was caring, kind, honest, and truthful, sometimes to a fault, and she had a memory like a steel trap. She was beautiful and witty, and she almost always had something of note to say about any subject. She had a strong sense of character and tried to instill in me the importance of being honest, straightforward, and punctual, that your word was your bond, and that you should never promise anything to someone you would be unable to honor. Her "pearls of wisdom," as I call them, have come to serve me well throughout my life.

I remember one day when I was very unhappy. I had a disagreement with some of my friends, and it was weighing heavily on me. For several days, I moped around the house. I am guessing my mother left me alone, thinking it would eventually resolve itself, but it did not. On the third or fourth morning, I can't remember which, she confronted me, saying, "We need to talk; what is the problem?" Everything came spilling out. She listened to every word I had to say, and then she said to me, "Honey, anyone can be miserable. It takes a little work to be happy, so don't forget that!" She said, "You have control over one person. Who do you think that is?" I thought for a second and finally answered, "Me," with a question in my voice. She said, "That is correct, and remember, no one can make you unhappy unless you allow them to. She suggested that when I felt this way, it was important to try to turn my unhappy thoughts around with thoughts that put a smile on my face. If I could not think of an incident or a person, I should try walking outside, looking at the beautiful flowers and sky, and thinking how wonderful the breeze felt on my face."

My mother was a very entertaining raconteur. One of her favorite stories she loved telling me was about Rose Masur, who was the Grand Dame of Jewish society in Monroe during the '30s and '40s. Miss Rose, as most folks called her, loved to entertain.

On the day of one of her luncheons, Miss Rose woke, not feeling well. She told the cook that she had planned to make the dessert, and since she was feeling poorly, she would order some things from the drugstore and have them deliver ice cream. She told the cook to make some pretty little parfaits with the ice cream and would be down in time to greet her guests for lunch. As the dessert was being served, whispers and giggles exploding into gales of laughter went around the table. The beautiful little sterling compotes of dessert consisted of a scoop of vanilla ice cream with chocolate sauce, a ring of whipped cream, and a glycerin suppository with a cherry on the top that was being placed before each guest.

You can't make it up!

Ground Rules

I realized very early that life with my mother was much more pleasant when I rocked with the punches instead of trying to buck the establishment. There was no doubt she ruled the roost and if she said no, it was not open for discussion. I remember when some of my friends planned to bike to Indian Mound to look for arrowheads. My mother thought it was much too dangerous and said no. I was heartbroken. The next thing I knew, she had organized a wonderful chaperoned biking excursion to Indian Mound I will never forget.

For the most part, my mother and I had a pretty happy relationship, although there were times when she said no, I thought she was being unfair. I would laugh and tell her to her face that she had "smotherly" love.

Years later, when Abry and I took the children to New Orleans to visit Mimi and Pawpaw, Abry was concerned about their safety. New Orleans, or "Sin City" as it was called, was a far cry from Shreveport, where the kids could ride their bikes almost anywhere. I told Abry we had nothing to worry about because the minute we walked through the door, everything was out of our control. We would "all" be living by Mimi's ground rules, and she would be in full control. We hadn't been in the house for five minutes when the kids, all excited, ran into the room and asked us if they could run down to the corner for an ice cream cone. Abry didn't miss a beat. He said y'all know the drill, "Go ask your grandmother; we have no say."

On this particular trip to New Orleans, Susan and Tab must have been around 8 and 11 years old when, one evening, Pawpaw said, "Let's go listen to some jazz music." At that time, you could still drive down Bourbon Street. We all piled in the car, and off we went. As we turned on Canal, Pawpaw said," Everybody, roll your windows down." As we turned onto Bourbon Street, strains of the blues were coming from all directions. This was Pawpaw's idea of listening to jazz. All the joints had their doors open, and there was either a stripper scantily dressed trying to coax tourists into their joints, hawkers offering a discount on the first drink and a free show, or a jazz musician blowing his horn. The kids were introduced to the real New Orleans at a very young age. Pawpaw, Abry, the kids, and I were loving it and my mother was about to have a hissy fit. I still remember my mother sitting in the car with her hands over her eyes. The kids still talk about that event to this day.

I think the outing served a very important purpose. Susan and Tab accepted the French Quarter as "just part of New Orleans" and not as some "forbidden fruit." Another favorite destination for the family was Café Du Monde, where we could sit on the patio and order café au lait and donuts. There was always some musical entertainment going on in the street. Life was good, and living was easy. Those were the days.

3201, as we called the place Mimi and Pawpaw lived, was built around a city block with a beautiful New Orleans-style courtyard in the center. Weather permitting, many homeowners would gather on the patio late afternoons for cocktail hour. My parents' home opened directly on to the patio, so when my mother was at home, she was always entertaining, fixing drinks and serving hors d'oeuvres to all the visitors. They named my mother "The Hostess of 3201." She wore her new title well.

Mimi and Pawpaw.

3201 was a little Peyton Place. Most of the time, everyone knew everyone else's business. This particular Saturday afternoon, the weather was beautiful, and there was a large gathering on the patio. People noticed a group of workers in white jump suits wheeling empty trolleys into the elevator and returning through the patio with TVs, lamps, rugs, and furnishings covered with tarps. There was a discussion about the fact that no one in the group knew of anyone who was moving out. My mother continued serving lemonade and cokes, and the men finally left with the last load. Shortly after, everyone returned to their homes to prepare for dinner. It was not too long after that all "Hell" broke loose when several of the couples found their homes had been burglarized right under their nose.

Bernie

My stepfather Bernie, or Pawpaw as Susan and Tab called him, was an amazing man. He had a photographic memory, and one of the things he did to entertain the children was to go through a deck of all 52 cards, one card at a time. When he had gone through the entire deck, the kids would call a number, and Pawpaw would tell them what the card was.

He was an avid Short Wave Radio operator. His call letters were W5IVF. He received an accommodation from the president for his volunteer service to the armed services. He would connect military personnel stationed in remote places without telephone service with loved ones they had not spoken to in months. He also did volunteer service during many of the hurricanes in areas where the power was out. For many years, out of the blue, he would receive a letter or a phone call of thanks for his dedicated service and help from someone whom he had connected with a wife or parents they had not been able to speak to in months.

As a kid, I remember Bernie on the radio; it felt like nonstop. Saying C Q, C Q, this is W5IVF. It made me crazy, thinking, will this ever stop? The house was small, and there was no place to get away from the constant racket. When Abry and I became engaged, one of the first things I thought about was, "Thank God! I will be getting away from the shortwave radio." Silly me, Abry had become fascinated with it and wanted to get his license so we could talk to my parents every day. Bernie helped him study for the test. Lo and behold,

I came home one day, and there Abry was, in our den, hooking up his radio. From that day forward until Pawpaw passed away, we spoke to my parents almost every day at 5:30 pm. Abry's call letters were K5LHW. If Abry happened to be a little late getting home, I would turn on the set and say, "W5IVF... this is K5LHW. Are you there?"

Television was just beginning to become the fashion. Bernie, being fascinated with anything new that was mechanical, decided to open a television store. We were the first people in Monroe to have a television set. The set was manufactured by Philco, and the screen was a sepia color. To promote business, my parents would invite different people over to watch a little TV in the evenings, hoping to sell a set. After a few months, my mother's cousin Patricia told my mother that she and Bernie had invited almost the entire town over to view the new contraption. However, she had not invited her own relatives. My mother and Bernie were getting very tired by now from watching TV every evening with company, but they knew this was something they had to do. They made a date, and Patricia and Alan came to the house. They turned on the set and settled down. Mother said all of a sudden, she woke up with a start, and Pat was standing over her and Bernie with her hands on her hips saying, "Well, when you are in someone's home, and one of the hosts falls asleep, it is bad, but when they both fall asleep then it is time to go home!" That was the end of the TV parties.

By this time, my mother and Bernie were living in New Orleans. Loyola University had purchased one of the first IBM computers, and Bernie was called into service to program the computer. The computer ran with programmed punch cards that were placed in slots in this huge gray metal monster of an electric box. It was Pawpaw's job to work out the punch cards so the correct program would print out of the box. I remember my mother complaining about the entire house being overrun with computer punch cards. He did such a great job that the university wanted him to give up his job with XOM and come to work for them managing the computer room. That was not going to happen. Years later, when Bernie retired, he decided to go back to school to get a law degree. When he enrolled at Loyola University, they told him he was accepted and did not have to take an entrance exam. Bernie and two of his friends were going to open their office together and call themselves "The Over the Hill Gang." Unfortunately, this dream never happened. One of Bernie's dreams did come true, though. He adopted me on his deathbed, and I became the daughter he had wanted me to be for so many years. My name was now Nell Bridge Wilenzick Cahn, and it was quite a mouthful.

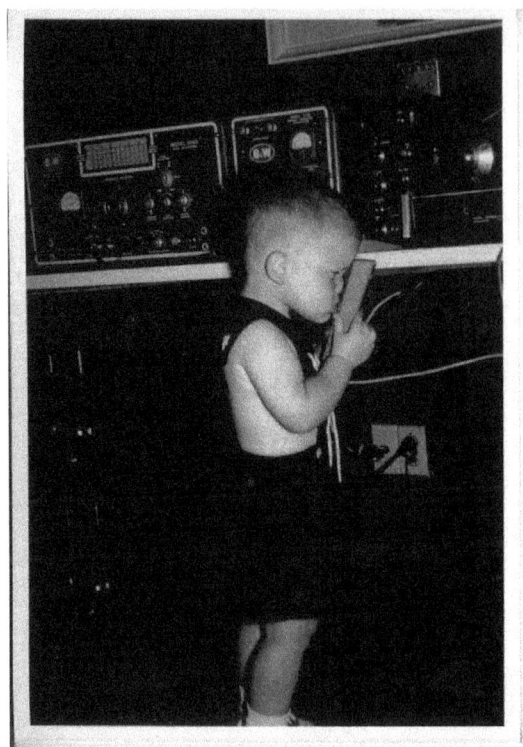

Tab playing with shortwave radio.

A New Life

I must have been around thirteen years old when my mother came into my room on Island Drive and told me that she and Bernie were going to be married and I would have a father. How wonderful it would be because we would have our own little home and a normal family life. Believe me, there was nothing ever normal about our family or our life. My mother told me I would always be her number one priority and that she was doing this for me as much as for her. She said that nothing would change because I would only have to answer to her. She would not let Bernie have any say in discipline or my upbringing. She told me he wanted to adopt me, but it would not happen unless I wanted it. The last thing I wanted was to change my name from Bridge to Wilenzick. That was a mouthful. She hoped I would come to love him because he loved me as if I were his own. Somehow, none of what she was saying was making much sense to me. I loved my home and my life, and I did not want to leave my home.

The die was cast!

They were married in December, and when they returned from their honeymoon, we moved into a little cottage on Fairview Avenue around the corner from the big house on Island Drive. At least it was within walking distance. Strangely enough, my life was so busy and full with school, Girl Scouts, and dancing lessons that I began to enjoy coming home to Fairview. It got to a point where my mother would have to insist that I go over and visit Grandma, Grandpa, and Aunt Ecca.

Bernie came from a large family. He had five brothers. One of them, Phillip, had passed away at a very young age. Uncle Harold, a dentist and colonel in the Air Force, was stationed in Japan. He and his wife, Janet, had two children, Linda and Melvin. Uncle Alex owned an exclusive tailor shop in Monroe, and his wife was named Nedra. Bernie's brother Mark and his wife Alma had one son, who was one year older than me. His name was Raymond, and he was brilliant. He loved magic and was quite a skilled magician. Raymond was also fascinated by chemistry and always had some experiments underway in his room, which he found entertaining. He had no social life to speak of, so one day, I took it upon myself to invite him over to the house to teach him how to dance. I had just gotten my braces off my teeth and was enjoying a big wad of chewing gum. I opened my mouth to say something, and the gum fell out and into the big wing chair in the living room. Raymond and I started laughing so hard that we were doubled over. We started to look for the gum and could not find it anywhere. Of course, that just made us laugh harder. Strange as it may seem, to my knowledge, we never found the gum. I never told my mother. It was many years later when Ray, as we called him then, told me I showed him a social life he never would have known if not for me.

Uncle Joe and Aunt Maxine lived in New Orleans. Their daughter, Carla, several years younger than me, was a very talented child, like a little wind-up doll who would sing and dance at her mother's command.

There were two half-sisters—Dorothy, a stenographer in New York, who was never married and was rarely visible at any family functions, and Gladys, married to Joe Dante, who lived in Winnsboro, Louisiana. Aunt Gladys and Uncle Joe had three boys: Selwyn, the oldest, and the twins, Morris and Jules, who were two years older than I was. Uncle Joe owned a retail store in Winnsboro. Visiting their home was always a blast. They were a game-playing family, and there was always plenty of action. Most weekends, there was always at least one Gin Rummy game in progress and either a Monopoly game or a game of Booray[5]. The twins played the piano, so we always had some song time. It was a new life for me, and I loved being a part of a large family with so many young people who enjoyed each other's company.

It was at Selwyn and June's wedding when I met Abry Cahn, my husband. Abry and Selwyn were Zeta Beta Tau (ZBT) fraternity brothers at LSU and, with two other students, shared a house in Baton Rouge, Louisiana. They named the house the "I'm A Goniff House." Abry was a groomsman, and June asked me to be a bridesmaid. I was a freshman at Neville High School, and Abry was a sophomore at LSU. I was fourteen, and Minette and I were still playing dolls, unbeknownst to our fellow classmates.

The wedding was at the Jung Hotel in New Orleans, and we planned to drive down the day before the wedding. Dresses for the bridesmaids were to ship to each of the girls two weeks before the wedding, giving adequate time for alterations. That did not happen. Instead, we would connect with our dresses in the ballroom at the hotel the day before the wedding. An alteration lady would meet us in the ballroom to do the necessary fittings. This turned into an absolute disaster as none of the dresses fit any of us. The dresses were gold satin with a huge stand-up collar. My dress was enormous. We were all running around trying other dresses, hoping to find one that fit better. Little did we know at this point that there was the possibility there might not even be a wedding. June had become very ill several days before and was in the hospital. We would not know until Saturday morning if the wedding would even take place. When the alteration lady finally arrived, she explained the situation and told us

---

[5] Booray, or Bourré, is a casino type game for four or more players. Played with a standard 52 playing card deck, in Booray Aces are high and 2s low. The objective of Booray is to win the most tricks out of 5 rounds.

there was plenty of time to fix all the dresses. She assured us that we would look perfect. June did make it out of the hospital for the wedding, although she sat in a chair during the ceremony. As I walked down the aisle, I noticed there was a handsome young man who could not take his eyes away from me. His name was Abry Cahn, and it was seven years later that we were married.

The reception broke up early because June had to return to the hospital. All the young folks were making plans to go out to the town. Abry had asked the cousins to talk to my parents so they would let me come. Aunt Janette's sister, Marilyn Rosenberg, who was engaged to Abry's roommate, Jack Kleban, talked to my parents and told them that she would take very good care of me if they would let me go. When they agreed, I was ecstatic and could not believe my ears. We went to Pat O'Brien's and several other joints in the quarter. I thought I had died and gone to Heaven. My drink of choice was always Coca-Cola. When the evening was over, Abry and I had vowed to keep in touch.

High School Days

School started after our return from Selwyn and June's wedding. To my great surprise, when I walked into my speech class, my teacher was none other than Marilyn Rosenberg, Aunt Janet's sister, whom I had double-dated with in New Orleans. Marilyn had returned to Monroe to teach at Neville while her fiancé, Jack, was completing his degree at LSU. Marilyn was bright and beautiful, and we had too much fun. I saw a lot of her not only at school but also at family functions. That class was my favorite. Abry and Jack were roommates, so Marilyn kept me posted on what was happening at LSU.

Marilyn was also head of the Tigerettes, the girl's marching pep squad at Neville. All eleven of the group were members. Neville's football team was the best in the state. We had a spirit that no other school could equal. The band and the pep squad followed the team to all the ball games. We marched and traveled together through all four years of high school.

The big social event for freshman girls at Neville was to receive an invitation to the rush party for Lambda Sigma Chi, the girl's sorority. Minette and I were the only two Jewish girls in our class, and we had no idea that no Jews had ever been invited to join. Antisemitism was running rampant in the country at the time. However, as strange as it may seem, we never had any exposure to that in Monroe. Our friends had always treated us as equals. When the invitations came out, Minette and I did not receive one for the rush party. It was a rude awakening, not just to us but also to our friends and their parents. Our friends and their parents got together and made a decision that the other girls would not go through the rush without us. They all refused the invitation. This was quite heartwarming.

Several weeks went by. One day in the mail, a new set of invitations arrived for a rush party for Lambda Sigma Chi[6]. Minette and I were on the invitation list, but this did not guarantee we would receive a bid to join. I remember the Smiths and my parents having numerous conversations about how to handle the situation. My mother and the Smiths were hesitant about my acceptance, as there was no certainty we would receive a bid just because we were invited to the rush party. Our parents did not want to see us get hurt. Bernie came to the rescue. He had such a level head and a wonderful way of viewing the world. He said, "Look, they have made the first move, and sometimes you just have to trust people. They would not have invited the girls to the party without the intention of giving them a bid to join." That night, it was with much excitement that Minette and I accepted their invitation and went to the rush party, knowing there were no guarantees. Bernie was right; we received a bid to join. Many situations similar to this one took place in other parts of the country, but luckily, ours was one with a happy ending. We were truly blessed to have unprejudiced, kind, and loving friends. I think we are indeed God's "chosen people."

A favorite pastime for the family was to sit on the front porch and visit when the weather was not too hot. Neighbors would stop over, and living was easy. Abry and I continued to correspond. Just like every other small town where everyone knew everyone else's business. One day, we were all sitting on the front porch, and Claud, our mailman, walked up and said, "Nell, you have a letter from Abry today." We laughed so hard we couldn't stop.

---

[6] My high school sorority.

Our neighbor, Mrs. Isbell, as I knew her, was crazy as a loon. She raised cats and had dozens of them. There were cats all over the place. When the weather was cold, and Bernie needed to go to his office, he could not start the car because some of the cats would be under the hood trying to keep warm. He would have to open the hood of his car and *shoo* them away; otherwise, he would have cat hair and parts flying all over the place. It was disgusting. I remember a long-running battle with my stepfather trying to get Mrs. Isbell to get rid of some of the cats. I never knew exactly what happened and did not want to know the particulars. But one day, all the cats were gone.

The summer of my junior year, Sally Archibald, my friend and art mentor, moved back to Houston so she could take care of her sick mother. Our new neighbors were Leila and Jim Ewing, a darling young couple with a new baby and a Catahoula Hound dog who loved me. Leila loved to play bridge and was anxious for Jim to learn how. My mother told her I was trying to learn the game. Also, she said if Jim were interested, she would call Miss Lilly Harrington, the grand dame of the bridge in Monroe, and see if she would be willing to give us lessons. A time was set, and Jim and I went to our first and last bridge lesson with Miss Harrington. The first thing she said was that the value of an Ace was four points.

Jim looked up and said, "What is an ace?"

We never went back!

The school was having a Valentine's Day dance, and I had the most magnificent dress. My date brought me a beautiful corsage with little red roses. As he helped me into the car and was getting ready to close the car door, Jim and Leila's dog, Big Blue, jumped into my lap and would not budge. My date had to get my parents, to get Leila and Jim, to come get the dog. When they finally got Big Blue to move, my hair and my dress were a mess, and half the roses had fallen off the corsage. This could be traumatic for some folks, but my mother and I always had a very bad habit of laughing at the wrong time. Once it was determined I was OK, my mother was laughing so hard she could

YOU CAN'T MAKE IT UP!

hardly stand up. This got everyone else "tickled," and none of us could stop laughing. A joint effort by Leila and my mother had me "patched back together" in no time. I do not know how she did it, but Leila had the roses stuck back on the corsage, and off to the dance we went.

I did not see Abry again until Marilyn and Jack's wedding in the summer of 1952. Once again, I was a bridesmaid, and he was a groomsman. He was still as handsome, and the chemistry was still there. My mother delivered a little sermon about the birds and the bees and the fact that there were good girls and bad ones. I had to take responsibility and respect myself since it was very tempting to indulge in a heated moment. Her parting shot was, "Just remember, when a man decides to take a wife, he does not want damaged goods." Also, she said, "Keep in mind, why should he buy the cow when the milk is free." Something must have "stuck" because when I walked down the aisle, I was still a virgin.

Where To From Here

We were entering our senior year in the fall of '52 with the realization that graduation was no longer a dream but a fact. It would not be very long before my friend and bridge partner, Shirley McDonald, would be going to school in St. Louis, Missouri; Minette and several of the other girls would be heading to LSU for college. I wanted desperately to go with them. I could see us being roommates, and life would be pretty much the same. My mother had different thoughts. She felt LSU was entirely too large and wanted me to go to a finishing school for girls as she and my aunt had done. Ward-Belmont, thank goodness, was no longer in existence.

Several schools sent representatives to Monroe to try to recruit us. There were three of us: Jo Marie Elliot, who had lived a very sheltered life and did not mix much socially; Susan Anderson, and yours truly. Susan and I decided to stick together and insist to our parents that we should go to the same school and be roommates. The two schools we were considering were Bryn Mawr and Stephens College.

The presentation from Bryn Mawr was very formal and quite impressive. There were also very strict academic requirements.

Stephens College was a much newer school, and the administration was working very hard trying to increase its enrollment. Both schools had very high ratings. The rep from Stephens College made a very impressive presentation. The school looked wonderful. There were classes in aeronautics. They had a great equestrian department equipped with up-to-date stables where the girls could bring their own horses, too. A very important feature for me was the department for dress design. The representative was leaving the next day, and one more meeting at 9:00 AM was set up with our parents. At that meeting with the representative, she made it clear we would be accepted as students and guaranteed a spot if we agreed to sign up within the next week. Bryn Mawr would offer us nothing until they saw our school records and thoroughly investigated the families.

Tab and Susan.

To all of us, Stephens College seemed a wonderful solution that would give us an outstanding education and keep us sheltered for at least another year. The decision was made. It was off to Columbia, Missouri, and Stephens College for the three of us.

Our senior year was one to be remembered. We all thought we were the best class that had ever graduated from Neville High School. To this day, I think we probably were. The football team won All-State that year, and our senior play, "*In the Good Ole Summertime*," was a roaring success. As time grew closer to graduation, big plans were being made for our Senior Prom. With the help and guidance of parents and school advisors, the theme for our prom was "The Wheel of Fortune," chosen from the 1953 hit song.

I had no steady high school beau. I had been brought up with the understanding from my family that I should never become too involved with anyone in high school because it was very important for me to marry within the Jewish faith. There were no Jewish boys in our class. Everyone was pretty much paired up into couples in our class, so I was very lucky to end up with a cute date for the prom. Frank Scalia, my neighbor and long-time friend, was dumped by his girlfriend, Leila Bess Kite, a couple of months before the prom. Frank and I had dated several times before he started going out with her. There was nothing serious, but we always had a lot of fun together. I loved to dance, and Frank was a terrific dancer. I was thrilled when he asked me to go to the prom.

As time progressed, my mother and I were extremely busy trying to get my wardrobe together for my year at Stephens College. Around the middle of July, I was informed that my friend Susan Anderson and roommate-to-be would not be attending Stephens College in the fall. According to the story, she and Wayne Woods had eloped. The real news was that she was pregnant. This left me in quite a pickle as I would be going a very long distance with no roommate. After many conversations with the school and guaranteeing they would place me with a compatible roommate, I agreed to venture forth as planned. It was a great disappointment that Susan would not be going with me. As all my friends were excited about heading to LSU together, the rude awakening came. The only child was once again alone, venturing off to a strange school hundreds of miles away from friends and family to find her way all by herself. For the first time in my life, I felt terribly alone.

As the summer wound down, the classy department store in Monroe, "The Palace," was going to have an off-to-college-style show. I was asked to model. Bob Hope with Les Brown and his "band of renowned" were hired by the Palace to narrate the show. Lots of publicity and my photo with Bob Hope in the newspaper was very exciting. I loved all the attention.

My college wardrobe was beginning to shape up. Columbia, Missouri, was going to be very cold. I was going to need something warmer than a cloth coat. My heart was set on a sheared Beaver coat, but the cost was prohibitive. We finally settled on a blond Muskrat. I never could stand that coat. I was ashamed of it. The funny thing was that when I came home for the Christmas holiday, it was freezing back in Columbia. I was so happy to have the coat. When I boarded the plane, I was sitting next to a man in a black suit. When we landed in St. Louis, and I started to leave the plane, my seatmate was frantically trying to brush himself off. He was covered with blond hair from the coat. It was obvious the pelts were defective and had evidently not been processed properly. How embarrassing. The Palace did refund the $400 my mother had paid for the coat.

I have been bogged down and unable to write for some time now, as this time in my life is probably one of the saddest. I knew it was going to be very difficult for me to revisit these memories. My parents were at the gate in Monroe waiting for me. When I saw their faces, I knew something was horribly wrong. My Cousin Shirley Kaplan Orkin, her husband, Jerry Orkin, and their two children were killed when a plane crashed into their home in Guam. Jerry was a doctor, and he was finishing his term of duty with the USAF. He was originally scheduled to be stationed in Germany. Aunt Clara thought that Germany would be so unsafe because of the unrest from the war that she begged Uncle David to contact Otto Passman, a State Senator, and a friend, and see if he could have any luck changing Jerry's tour of duty. They were so thrilled when this came about because Shirley and the kids would be able to join Jerry in Guam. Had he gone to Germany, they would have had to remain stateside until he returned. The family was inconsolable. I will take to my grave the picture of those four coffins, the two big ones and the two baby ones. Our family would never be the same.

When I returned to Stephens College after the holidays, it was not with a Muskrat coat but Shirley's exquisite leopard coat that "Big Mama," Aunt Clara's mother, had given her for her twenty-first birthday.

The remainder of the year was relatively uneventful. My roommate Marcia Julian from Miami was quite a character; we were both in the school of dress design, and we really had a good time together. Neither one of us had anyone very interesting to date. Marcia said, "We still had to keep shopping because you never knew what was right around the corner." Neither one of us ever met anyone that year that was worth mentioning. Abry and I continued to correspond, and, on occasion, he would phone. Marilyn Rosenberg, my speech teacher at Neville, and Jack Kleban, Abry's roommate and best friend from LSU days, were finally tying the knot in Monroe in June. Abry and I were both excited that we would once again be bridesmaid and groomsman in the same wedding.

As our first year at Stephens College came to an end and I said goodbye to Marcia and our two suite mates with hugs and kisses, we had big plans to return in the fall to our same wonderful dorm, "Hatcher Hall." The dorm was in the location where the library now stands. Living there was like living in a grand mansion, and we all loved it and looked forward to our return.

Nell on the firetruck.

Bama Days

I had only been home from Stephens College for a couple of weeks when I received a phone call from my roommate, Marcia Julian, saying that she would not be returning for the fall semester. She said she met someone and would be attending the University of Miami in the fall. I was once again on the horns of a dilemma of what to do without a roommate.

My childhood friend Charles Massur was attending the University of Alabama (UoA) and convinced me that "Bama" was where it was at. The UoA was known to be the playground of schools in the south. Charles's mom, Miss Ethel, had remarried and moved back to Monroe from Tuscaloosa. He said he would be driving back and forth and would be more than happy to have my company for the ride. My parents thought a quick trip to Tuscaloosa to check out the school would be the thing to do before I made any decision. A trip was planned for the next weekend when Charles and Miss Ethel were planning to go. They would be able to show me the ropes and introduce me to some of the locals. The minute I saw the University, I loved it and couldn't wait to put in my application. We were really cutting it close if I wanted to get there in time for Rush Week. My grades were satisfactory, so my acceptance came back immediately; I was Alabama-bound and couldn't wait.

*****

Tuscaloosa was a beautiful town, and it reminded me a lot of Columbia, Mo. Even though I was entering my sophomore year, I would be living in the Tutwiler dormitory, which was housing for freshman girls living on campus. My parents helped me move in and saw that I was settled before they headed back to Monroe.

In 1954, none of the dormitories had private telephones in the rooms. There was one hall phone for the entire floor. I had just finished unpacking when I heard someone outside my door yelling, "Nell, some guy is on the hall phone asking for you." I had no clue who would possibly be calling me. When I said "Hello?" the voice on the other end introduced himself as Stan Bloom. I remembered I had been introduced to him by Miss Ethel on the previous trip to Tuscaloosa. He told me he was at my service and would love to show me the town before I became involved with all the school activities and rush. After serving in the army, Stan returned to Tuscaloosa to manage their family business, Bloom's Department Store. Stan had evidently done his homework because he knew I played golf and that I loved to dance. Our outing began and ended at the Tuscaloosa Country Club, of which he was a member. I thought we would probably go inside and have a coke or a bite to eat, but I never saw the inside of the clubhouse. He wanted to show me the golf course. I had dressed in my best little sundress and some fancy sandals, which were not appropriate for walking the course. It was so hot that I thought I was going to expire. After about the fourth hole, I begged off and told him I had to return to the dorm to meet up with some of the girls for dinner. Stan invited me to a dinner dance at the country club on Saturday night, which I refused. Rush was starting the next day, and I was excited about getting involved in campus life. I really didn't care if I ever saw Stan again. I had the feeling he was shopping for a wife and was not being terribly subtle about it. I thought he was too old, although, thinking back, he probably was only a couple of years older than Abry. Stan gave me a card with his telephone number and told me that if I needed anything, I would know how to contact him. If it hadn't been for the fact that he owned a very impressive store, I probably would have thrown his number out the minute I returned to the dorm. Instead, I tucked it away, just in case.

The first day of rush was a madhouse. We were invited to each of the sorority houses on campus for a short visit. At the end of the day, we were given a card to fill out with our choice of three sororities, placing them in the order of our preference. I thought this was going to be a simple task for me because there were only three Jewish sororities: Sigma Delta Tau (SDT), Alpha Epsilon Phi (AEPhi), and the third one, for the life of me, I can't remember what it was. I was so wrong. What I did not realize until a short time before I left for Alabama was that my mother had gone to LSU after Ward-Belmont and had pledged SDT. AEPhi was formed years after SDT and was fast becoming the most popular Jewish sorority on a number of college campuses. There was much speculation as to the best Jewish sorority on campus. Almost everyone from Tuscaloosa thought SDT was the number-one choice at Bama. The sorority had been on campus for years, and their house was far more impressive than the AEPhi house. I was torn, but I finally chose AEPhi because most of the girls I was friendly with were either already AEPhis or knew they were going to pledge AEPhi. I was given bids to both sororities, and I must admit, it was very hard saying no to SDT.

Soon after the bids came out, all the sororities held open houses to introduce the new pledges. The members of the Jewish fraternities were also invited to welcome the new girls.

The evening wasn't underway very long before one of the guys asked me to dance. He introduced himself as Harold Bowman Blach lll, President of ZBT Fraternity from Birmingham, Alabama. Harold was very cute and very pompous. Harold was a senior and would be leaving for the Air Force at the end of the year. I later found out he was also known as the best Jewish catch on campus. His family owned a fabulous department store in Birmingham. We made a date for the following weekend when ZBT would be hosting a mixer for all the new AEPhi pledges. Fairly quickly, we became an item. I was

Harold's choice of dates for most of the intown football games and some of the out-of-town games if they weren't too far away. My social life had taken off, and I was having a blast. Abry was in the army and stationed at Bethesda, Maryland. I had not heard from him in ages.

A few weeks before Yom Kippur, Harold invited me to Birmingham to stay in his home and attend services. Everyone seemed to think this was a pretty serious invitation. I honestly thought it was something a friend would do for a friend who could not get home for the holiday. It was also Harold's birthday, and his parents were giving him a new Oldsmobile as a present. We were to stop at the Oldsmobile place on the way in to pick up the car. They were expecting us to be there in time for dinner. It had not been very long after we left the car agency that the new car stopped completely. We were on one of the busiest streets in Birmingham. It did not take very long to find the problem with the car; we were out of gas. When they serviced the car, they failed to check the tank. His folks were fit to be tied when we finally arrived. His father was on the phone screaming at the car salesman; I remember him hollering into the telephone, "Listen, you SOB, the next time I sell you a suit, I'm leaving the zipper out of the pants." That cracked me up, but nobody else laughed. By now, it was too late to make the evening service, and we had ended up having dinner and attending the morning services.

I was dressed in a beautiful Paula Parnes suit with a little white blouse embroidered with blue flowers. The first thing his mother said was, "Where in the world did you get that suit?" I told her the Palace in Monroe, Louisiana. In a very accusatory voice, she said, "I bought that same suit for Alice. You know Harold's sister." I don't know why I said "Thank you," but I realized later that she had not given me a compliment. On the way back to Tuscaloosa, I realized I did not have what you would call a warm and fuzzy feeling towards his parents. I was reasonably certain the feeling was mutual with his mother. I went to Birmingham with Harold on a couple of other occasions and stayed in their home. Once, when Alabama was playing Auburn in Birmingham, I felt his parents were always cordial but not particularly overjoyed to see me. I was never sure if his mother even knew my name. I did find out years later that Harold's mother and father had contacted the Rabbi in Monroe for information about my family and me.

Harold's best friend, Jack Held, was finishing his senior year in law school. Jack and his wife Evelyn loved to play bridge. Whenever our study loads permitted, we would go over to their home and spend the evening playing bridge at their kitchen table.

School was out in May, so I headed back to Monroe. Harold graduated and joined the Air Force. He was in training camp and, as he put it, learning how to fly a desk. It was around the end of June when I received a call from my friend Charles Masur, who told me that Harold was engaged to be married to Joanie Bain from Pine Bluff, Arkansas. I was in total shock that Harold had not had the courtesy to tell me himself. I did not have a clue he was even dating anyone else. I was absolutely devastated and felt totally betrayed. Charles came and picked me up and took me to the Rendezvous Drive-in for French fries, a Coke, and a good cry on his shoulder. What a good friend he was.

Surprise of surprises: Abry called a few weeks later and told me he was coming to Monroe over the 4th of July for a get-together with some of his LSU buddies and hoped I could go out with him. I was thrilled, and my remorse over Harold was short-lived. Abry and I had a grand time, and yes, the magic was still there. In the fall, he would finish his stint in the Army and return to Shreveport. Abry was an electrical engineer and would be going to work in the family business "Cahn Electric."

In late August, I headed back to Alabama for rush. I would be living in the sorority house.

My Dance Card was Empty

I returned to school that fall, knowing my social life would be taking a drastic change. I would be returning with no plans and no dates for anything. My friend Charles came to my rescue. He called and said, "Just say so if you would rather not do this. A good friend and fraternity brother, Bernard Lobel, who graduated several years ago, will be in town this weekend. If you don't have plans, I thought you two might hit it off. Our fraternity is having a Bermuda Shorts party on Saturday night. What do you say?" I was thrilled to accept.

The evening came, and I was all decked out in my new little Bermuda short outfit, thinking I looked pretty cute. My date arrived, and I pranced down the stairs to find him standing there like he had just stepped off the runway as the best-dressed man of the year. Bernard was wearing a navy suit and a beautiful necktie. I wanted to disappear and arrive in a great-looking dress and heels. I said, "I thought we were going to a Bermuda Shorts party at the fraternity house. Let me go change." He said, "We are, but I don't wear Bermuda shorts, just not my thing." Then he said, "We are already late. You don't need to change as you will be dressed like everyone else." It was a miserable evening, and it was perfectly obvious that he had realized that coming back to a college function on a blind date was a big mistake. We did not tarry very long. Bernard asked me if I cared to have a bite to eat before going back to the sorority house, and I declined; I couldn't get back fast enough.

Several days later, Abry called to see if I enjoyed my date and the party. I told him about Bernard arriving dressed in a suit and tie and what a miserable evening it was. At that point, Abry said, "Poor Bernard, I hope you weren't too hard on him about not wearing Bermuda shorts. You know he has a wooden leg." Abry went into detail about how difficult it was when Bernard was growing up to keep the artificial leg properly fitted so he would not walk with a limp. He told me that his parents would have to take him to have the leg adjusted every few months. I felt so bad for him—I was almost in tears. I guess Abry thought I knew he was joking. It was years later that I found out Bernard no more had a wooden leg than I did. Abry was just being funny. Would I ever learn? Probably not!

Classes started, and my life got so busy with my studies that I didn't have much time to think about dating. I also worked on doing an ad layout for The Psionian, the college newspaper. Football season was starting, and there was a competition between all the sororities and fraternities for the best-decorated house. The previous year, I was asked to plan the design for the ZBT fraternity house, and we won. I was really surprised when I received a call from Stanley Klein, president of ZBT at the time, and he asked me if I would please help them again. I was happy to accept that one of my passions was being able to design and be creative. We came up with a plan to make the front of the fraternity house "The Tums Factory." The Bama elephant is placing the injured MSU bulldog on a belt that moves into the Tums factory and comes out on the other side in a Tums wrapper. The belt moves him into a Tums truck. It wasn't even close; ZBT won hands down for the second year.

Stanley asked me if I would be his date for homecoming weekend. I liked him a lot and was happy to accept. It was an extremely funny situation, though. Stanley had bought Harold Blachs car when he graduated the previous year. The big joke around the fraternity house was that Stanley had Harold's old car and was now trying to get his old girlfriend. We had a really good time that weekend and enjoyed the excitement of our accomplishment. That was as far as it went. We never had another date.

A few weeks passed, and out of the blue, I received a phone call from none other than Stan Bloom. He invited me to a dinner dance at the Country Club the following Saturday night. I was happy to accept. I had beautiful cocktail clothes I had never put on my back, and it was really a lot of fun getting all dressed up. The club had a wonderful orchestra, and we had a grand time dancing. It had been a long time since I had had so much fun. Stan sent me flowers and candy, and I loved the attention.

Campus Unrest: 1955-1956

On June 29, 1955, the National Association for the Advancement of Colored People (NAACP) secured a court order preventing the University of Alabama (UoA) from rejecting the admission of Autherine Lucy and her friend, Pollie Meyers. The atmosphere on campus and in the town was one of anger with the forced acceptance of the first black female students to be admitted on campus.

Pollie Meyers decided to get married so that Autherine Lucy would be coming to the university alone.

The fall semester ran rather smoothly, even with the anticipation of the arrival of the new student. Lucy would not be entering college until after the first of the year.

When we returned from Christmas break, signs had been placed around the campus, "Keep Bama White" and "White People only." The atmosphere around the town and on campus was one of frustration and anger.

It was Feb3, 1956, when we started seeing a drastic change in the atmosphere. There were massive numbers of people on campus, and it was obvious they were not students. Most were poorly dressed men in workmen's clothes, probably the mill workers from intown.

The route to and from the sorority house to class was across the Square with the bell tower. Everything was fine going to my 2:00 P.M.

class, but two hours later, when I was returning, all "Hell" was breaking loose. There was a large group of male protesters carrying signs and ranting "Keep Bama White" in the middle of the quadrangle, and this was the only way back to the sorority house where I lived. I put my head down and just kept walking as if nothing was happening. There were news reporters from all over the world with their cameras rolling as they followed me, trying to get an interview. I just kept walking. When I finally got past all the protesters and reporters, I was shaking, and I remember I ran the remainder of the way to the sorority house. As soon as I walked through the front door, someone yelled, "Nell, your mom is on the telephone, hurry up."

The minute I said "Hello," my mother, who was, for the most part, very mild-mannered, was screeching over the phone, saying, "You are all over the national news. What in the world were you doing in the middle of a race riot? Don't you know they are rioting on the University of Alabama campus, protesting the arrival of Autherine Lucy?" It seems that my old roommate from Stephens College, Marcia Julien, in Miami, called my mother in New Orleans, telling her to turn on the TV while I was on national news. I was in class and had absolutely no idea that things had turned so violent on campus. Actually, the protesters where I walked were noisy, but thank goodness, not violent. However, I understand there were some on campus throwing rocks at the car that Autherine Lucy was in. The president of the university made the decision immediately that there was no way they could keep Lucy safe, and she must be removed from campus and not be allowed to return. Once she left, it was amazing how fast everything returned to normal.

Bogged Down

I was carrying a heavy schedule and was on an overload. I was taking a Chemistry class with a lab twice a week and an Economics class that I was flunking. I had never failed a course, but I felt reasonably sure it was going to happen with this one. I just could not get it.

Stan and I continued to date. I loved being able to dress up for dinner either at the Country Club or the one or two nice restaurants in town, or sometimes a dinner with his mother at their home. On Saturday, when the Country Club was holding a dinner dance, I was invited to check out of the sorority house and spend the night at their home so there would be no curfew. This was always a treat. Their home was magnificent, and I loved the guest room I stayed in, with its huge four-poster bed that was so tall there were steps to get in and out. Breakfast was brought to me in bed by their housekeeper, and I was treated like royalty. I think I truly fell in love with the elegance of my surroundings.

Valentine's Day arrived, and with it, a bouquet of red roses and a huge and beautifully wrapped box from Stan that was delivered to the sorority house. All the girls gathered around, waiting while I unwrapped my present. By the way, Stan also owned a clothes manufacturing business.

In the box was a little white embroidered detachable collar and a pair of Bermuda shorts. With the present was a handmade card in the shape of a heart that read:

"*From your neck to your behind,*

will you be my valentine?"

Love,

Stan.

I thought the gift and card were cute, but looking back many years later, I am certain I did not give him the response he was hoping for.

Easter vacation would be coming up shortly, and I had made plans to ride back to Monroe with Charles. Abry called me and said he would be visiting his old LSU buddies that weekend in Monroe, and he hoped I didn't have plans. He wanted to take me to the dance at the Country Club on Saturday. I was excited about getting to see him; it had been so long.

Stan was leaving for New York on a buying trip and would be there during Easter vacation. He took me to dinner the night before he left. During dinner, I remember him saying he wanted to do a little personal shopping in New York that involved me. He said he would like to buy me a ring while there. I think I was speechless because I made no verbal response. What I do remember is making an embarrassed giggle. The evening ended on a pleasant note. Stan walked me to the door, kissed me on the forehead, and he told me to have a great vacation and that he would see me when I returned to school the following week.

I had not been home very long when I received a phone call from the house mother at the AEPhi house telling me that the basement had flooded. My trunk, with all my clothes and belongings I had not brought home, was ruined. We would have to evacuate the sorority house for repairs. Everyone living in the house would be looking for a place to live for the remainder of the year. I realized I was not upset. In fact, I think I was overjoyed; I was flunking Economics, and I was sick of school. I was over my head in the relationship with Stan and knew I would have to face that when and if I returned to school.

Abry arrived the Friday evening before Easter to have a get-together with all his old LSU buddies. We had plans for dinner on Saturday before the dance at the Country Club. I was so excited I could hardly wait. During dinner, Abry said, "I have to ask you this: how serious are you about this guy from Tuscaloosa?" I remember laughing and saying, "He is definitely more serious than I am. He wants to buy me a ring." Abry said, "I always thought we would get married; I was just waiting until you finished school to ask you?" I said, "Is this a proposal?" Abry thought a second and said, "I guess so." I said, "Then I accept." Abry said, "Let us get out of here and tell our folks we are engaged."

Big excitement, we went back to the house and told my parents, then we called Abry's parents in Shreveport and his sister and brother-in-law to tell them our news. When things finally settled down, Abry and I arrived at the Country Club dance as the newly engaged couple. All of Monroe was a buzz.

Abry Cahn Sr (Pops) and Janice (Honey).

In all the excitement, I had completely forgotten about Stan. On Sunday afternoon, our friends gathered at our house to celebrate our engagement with champagne. Amidst all the commotion, someone suddenly said, "Nell, you have a long-distance phone call from some guy named Stan. By the way, he wants to know if the news of your engagement is true." When I answered, I made some feeble excuses about him being in New York and being unable to contact him. I apologized for him having to hear the news from someone else. He wished me a good life, and I reciprocated the sentiment.

It was now goodbye, Bama.

Shreveport, here I come!

Nell and Abry

June 23, 1956

Abry and I were married at the Bayou Desiard Country Club in Monroe, Louisiana, with a small gathering of approximately 100 relatives and extended family members. My mother summed it up: the Cahn side of the family crawled out from under the rocks in Little Rock and left no stone unturned.

The weekend was quite festive, with lunches, brunches, and barbecues.

My mother felt she had to keep the wedding small because of the expense. None of our friends were invited. Abry couldn't have cared less, and I was so excited about getting married that I left all the arrangements to my mother. On the day of our wedding, my best friend Minette came to the Country Club to see me in my bridal gown. It was then that I realized what a terrible mistake we had made not insisting that our close friends be included. Well, life goes on, and believe it or not, 62 years later, my girlfriends are still speaking to me, and only occasionally, it will come up in the conversation that one will say, "I can't believe your mother would not invite us to the wedding."

The time had now arrived for me to walk down the aisle. The beautiful music and the first strains of the wedding march began to echo in the room. The club was supposed to be closed for our blessed event. However, several of the high school kids had somehow gotten into the clubhouse and plugged in the jukebox just as I started down the aisle. Loud and clear through the sound system blared Teresa Brewer's newest song, "*Amarillo*" (not "Boll Weevil," which is an old blues song), and this is the music that accompanied me down the aisle. My mother, who was already seated, tried to jump up to run and tell them to cut off the jukebox, but thank goodness the photographer, Derwood Griffith, was able to take care of the situation. By then, I was poised at the altar (not "Alter," which is a typo), waiting for the Rabbi to start the ceremony.

A nice little reception that I barely remember followed. Soon, it was time to make our getaway to the airport. Howard, one of the loyal employees of the club, was driving the getaway car. The trip to the airport went very well except for a few cans, old shoes, and a cowbell tied to the bumper of the car. Our flight to Dallas was supposed to depart at 9:00 PM. We were to spend the night at the beautiful new Hilton Hotel in the bridal suite and then off to a blissful two weeks in Hawaii via San Francisco.

After we checked in for our flight with our little box of sandwiches, bits of wedding cake, and a bottle of champagne, we were anxiously awaiting the boarding time. Finally, it was time to take our seats on Delta's DC6. We sat on the runway for what seemed a very long period before the pilot came on the PA system to alert us to the fact that the hydraulic fluid had leaked out of the plane, which meant the landing gear would not work when he tried to land the plane in Dallas. It was now 10:30 pm and hot as the devil. An announcement came over the loudspeaker asking all passengers to deplane while they tried to locate an engineer to fix the problem. This turned out to be an exercise in futility. My goodness, we were in Monroe on a Saturday evening.

By 11:30 A.M., the airline gave up the task and decided to put everyone up at hotels for the remainder of the night. The problem we faced was that all the wedding guests would be staying at the Virginia Hotel and the Francis Hotel, so staying at one of those was out of the question.

The nice attendant who was helping us suggested the Broadmoor Motel on Desiard Road, which is not too far from the airport. This seemed like a good idea at the time, so we went off to the Motel in our Yellow Cab. As soon as we arrived, the desk clerk ran out to the taxi to register us. As the cab driver began unloading our nine pieces of luggage, plus a Neiman Marcus hatbox, a bottle of champagne, and a sack of sandwiches, the motel night clerk turned pale. No one had ever checked into the motel with such luggage. Business was really bad if the motel didn't have 100 guests on a Saturday night.

The night clerk was not overjoyed to fill the room with someone who was spending the entire night as he could only rent the room once. We finally got all the luggage crammed into the room and flopped down to polish off our wedding feast. Abry seemed to be very busy doing something, so finally, I said, "What are you doing?" "Setting up the tripod so we can have a little photo shoot in our bridal finery." My God, that was the last thing I had in mind, but we do have a beautiful photo album with wonderful photographs of our wedding night at the Broadmoor Motel.

I know you think this is the end of this saga of the honeymoon, and it would be great if it were only so. Little did we know, we had only just begun.

After a sumptuous breakfast feast of free Southern Maid donuts, we called both of our parents to tell them we were still in Monroe. Our flight would be leaving around noon and if they would like to pick us up at the Broadmoor Motel for another sendoff, we would be ever so grateful. After more hugs and kisses, we arrived at the airport and checked in at the counter, only to find out that the ventilation system was out on the plane, and there would be no air conditioning from Monroe to Dallas. It was only 103 degrees.

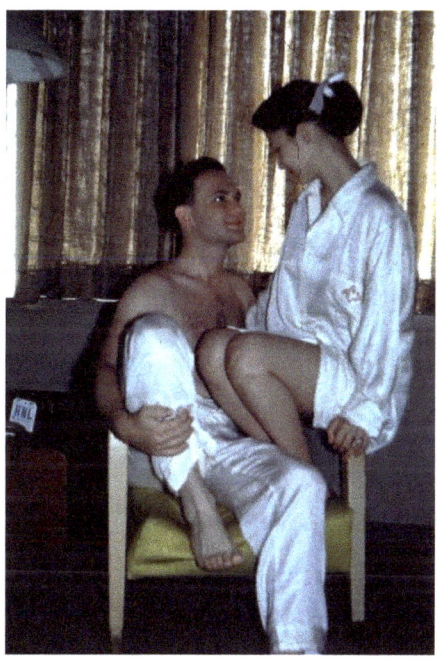

Abry and Me at Broadmoor Motel on our wedding night.

We had no other choice but to take the flight because we couldn't afford to miss our connecting flight from Dallas to San Francisco. Finally, we arrived in Dallas, and I don't think either of us had a dry stitch of clothing on our bodies. I rushed to the ladies' room to try to repair the damage. My hat was on crooked, I had lost one of my gloves, and my clothes looked as if I had slept in them. I took off my jacket and washed under my armpits with a paper towel, dried off as best I could, and still clutching my Neiman Marcus hatbox, I headed back to the terminal to find Abry. When I finally located Abry, he was chatting with a group of people from Shreveport who turned out to be Rae and Mandy Selber, Peggy and Aaron Selber, and a few others whose names I can't recall. Abry said, "Come on over, honey, they're anxious to meet the new bride." They all looked so cool, fresh, and beautifully dressed, while I looked like the poor, wilted violet. If I could have turned around and fled, I would have. This was not a very promising introduction to Shreveport society. We bid farewell with promises of getting together when we all returned from our separate adventures.

Abry and I headed to our gate in great anticipation of our red-carpet Pan Am flight to San Francisco. It was a beautiful sight to behold. There actually was a red carpet from the terminal to the Pan Am plane. The pilot and flight attendants were lined up in their crisp uniforms to welcome us aboard. We finally felt as if we were going on our honeymoon. We departed on time, and drinks were served immediately. All seemed to be great with the world when suddenly, a lot of activity erupted with the stewardess running up and down the aisles. Shortly after, the pilot came over to the loudspeaker and announced that there would be an emergency landing in Albuquerque, New Mexico. A man was having a heart attack and needed to be taken to a hospital. The pilot assured us we would only be detained for one hour. We would still be in San Francisco in plenty of time to check into the St. Francis Hotel and have a wonderful dinner and evening. It took a little longer than an hour, more like two, before we finally got clearance for our departure.

At last, we were on our way. There was an announcement that dinner would be served shortly. A tray with the most beautiful filet arrived, and I realized I was starving. As I dug into my steak for the first bite, I glanced out the window just in time to see the engine on the starboard side stop. "Yikes…Honey! Honey!" I said, "The engine just went out." Abry was engrossed in his food, and without looking up, he said, "Honey, don't worry, this is a big plane with three other engines; we'll be fine."

The pilot once again came over to the PA and announced that we would be making an emergency landing in Winslow, Arizona. He did not want to risk going over the mountains with only three engines. He also said, "We would be landing on a dirt runway, and there would not be a generator large enough to keep the power running." Each person would be responsible for getting their own luggage off the plane. We were told to finish dinner on the plane and then set about the task of retrieving our luggage. By that time, everyone knew we were on our honeymoon. As Abry was getting our luggage, the pilot said to him, "Well, son, this is something you can tell your grandchildren." Abry said, "At this rate, we aren't going to have any children."

There was no terminal building at this airport, only one room with a ticket counter, a dozen folding chairs, a cold drink machine, and one bathroom.

We collected our luggage, all nine pieces plus the Neiman Marcus hatbox I was still hanging on to. We found a nice spot under a tree with no leaves and staked our claim. The pilot made the announcement that Pan Am had located a plane in Las Vegas that they would send to us as soon as it had been serviced and maintenance had checked it out. The plane should be in Winslow in about six and a half hours. We were counting the time to load our luggage, which would put our departure time for San Francisco at approximately 2:00 AM.

Six and a half hours sure was a long time to be sitting in the middle of the Painted Desert. There was a little boy around three years old who kept running around in circles, looking up and crying, "Where's the plane?" Abry looked at me and said that's exactly what he felt like doing. Well, we have now missed our wonderful evening in San Francisco and our stay at the St Francis Hotel. Our only hope now would be to arrive in San Francisco, and if everything went off as scheduled at this point, we could possibly arrive at the hotel by 7:00 AM, and that would give us enough time to take a nice hot shower, catch a few hours of shut-eye before leaving on our flight to Hawaii. We were certainly overdue for some good luck. When we finally saw the lights of the plane approaching, everyone began to cheer. We loaded up in record time, and when we finally landed at the San Francisco airport, we were a pretty sorry group of hot, hungry, and tired folks who were very thankful to be safe.

Hawaii

I wish I could say that once we arrived in Hawaii, everything was perfect, but it was far from perfect. Our room was not made up, so they tried to humor us with Mai Tais and pretty girls doing the hula. An hour later, when we were finally taken to our room, we were both totally exhausted and, I must admit, a bit tipsy from the rum. Abry and I both ran for the bed and did not wake up until after dark. We managed to pull ourselves together in time for our dinner reservation at the Royal Hawaiian Hotel dining room.

Abry had ordered a fine bottle of wine, and when the Sommelier arrived at the table to open the bottle and make the formal presentation, he offered the first taste to Abry for approval. Abry, being the practical joker he was, told me later that it took every ounce of self-control he had not to grab his throat and spit the wine on the floor. He said this was something he had always dreamed of doing.

The next day, we both woke totally rejuvenated and raring to go. All the elements were right. It was a gloriously sunny day, and the water was crystal clear. Abry had donned his bathing suit and was anxious to head for the beach. His lifetime dream was to learn to ride the surf. Trying to ride a surfboard was not one of my ambitions in life, so I opted to watch. Poor Abry spent the better part of the day on his stomach, paddling out on the surfboard, waiting for another wave. I guess it never occurred to either of us that his "Lilly" white skin was being fried by the sun. We returned to the room, and much to our horror, Abry was in such pain from the sunburn that he could not sit down. We had the hotel contact a doctor who was very sympathetic and told us how many of these cases of tourists he had seen in the past few days who did not have a clue how damaging too much sun could be. He gave Abry some salve and something for the pain and told him he would be spending a lot of time on his stomach for the next few days.

Fortunately for me, my high school friend and bridge partner Shirley McDonald was going to summer school at the University of Hawaii. Shirley came to the hotel several times, and we had lunch and dinner together while Abry was convalescing. At this point, being with Shirley was the highlight of my honeymoon.

On the fourth day, Abry was finally able to navigate. He said he thought he would be able to dress for dinner that evening. One item in his trousseau was a pair of white silk pajamas. He thought that if he put on the bottoms of the silk PJs before he put on his slacks, the back of his legs would not hurt when he was seated. Off to dinner we went. We were sitting at the table for a while when we both looked down at the same time to see Abry's white silk pajama bottoms hanging out from below the leg of his slacks resting in a puddle on top of his shoes. Laughing, Abry said, "Those folks at the table next to us staring are probably saying, look that poor guy with his PJs hanging out below his pants. He definitely looks like the ever-ready bridegroom."

Fortunately, the remainder of our trip was perfect, and we both vowed that we would return someday.

On our return home, we were saddened to hear the news that Grandpa Kaplan had passed away.

Return from the Honeymoon

Abry and I returned from our honeymoon to our second-floor, one-bedroom apartment in Centenary. The apartment was painted a dark beige color, which was depressing. We had a king-size bed with no headboard, a card table in the living room, and two folding chairs. Even though I had majored in Home Economics in high school, I knew nothing about homemaking. Before our wedding, I had no interest in picking out a trousseau, leaving all of that up to my mother. My mother loved the color turquoise; all our bath towels were in turquoise, gray, and pink. We had a dozen of each monogrammed by hand. The pink towels were monogrammed with turquoise, the gray towels with pink, and the turquoise towels with gray. To complete the sets, we also had a dozen washcloths and a dozen hand towels. It took over 25 years to finally use them up. They weren't exactly compatible with the beige walls. We were young and happy, and things like that didn't seem very important.

Imy Marcus, who was Abry's best friend, had also returned to Shreveport with his new bride. The Marcus's owned the furniture store across the street from Cahn Electric. Abry and Imy had coffee every morning and couldn't wait to introduce their new wives. Imy's wife was Harriette Jacobson from Memphis, Tennessee. Harriette came from a very large family of two older brothers and two sisters. Harriette had an aunt named Tootsie who taught her style and appreciation of very expensive clothes and shoes. Harriette and I immediately became fast friends; we were inseparable. I learned from her how to put myself together with a complete outfit from purses, belts, scarfs, and the perfect pair of Herbert Levine shoes. We might have only one outfit in our closet, but when we walked out the door, we looked like we had stepped out of a bandbox.

Harriette was about three months pregnant when we first met. Baby Anne was born in September. Pops and I found out the day Anne was born that we were going to be parents in May. After a lengthy recovery from Anne's birth, Harriette called one day and said she and Imy hoped we could have an evening out together like old times before baby. She invited us over to see baby Anne, and we made plans to go out for a fancy dinner.

Abry and I arrived around 5:30 to view the new child, who was screaming her head off because she had just finished eating and had colic. We waited while they each took turns walking the floor until Anne fell asleep, and then we were finally able to be on our way. Imy and Harriette were living at Madison Park Apartments at the time. Harriette told Imy and Abry to go out the kitchen door to the garage, and Imy would drive their car and pick us up in front of the apartment. Harriette and I locked up and were standing on the curb waiting for the men to come around and pick us up when Harriette said, "Thank God! Finally, we are out of there. I'm so excited about our evening out." Suddenly, the realization hit me. I looked at Harriette and said, "Harriette, who is staying with the baby?"

"Oh my God!" Well, that was the end of that. We were laughing so hard we could hardly stand up. So much for our fancy dinner and night out. The fellows picked up hamburgers and brought them back to the apartment. We spent the remainder of the evening laughing about what idiots we all were and how unprepared we were for parenthood.

Coming of Age

August 12, 1956, was my twenty-first birthday, and I would be eligible to vote. My birthday fell on a Sunday that year, so Abry suggested I wait until Tuesday to register because it would not be as crowded. I was so excited I could hardly wait.

I remember my parents going to vote, and I do remember vague conversations about the up-and-coming new Republican party and the fact that it was gaining momentum in the area. Other than that, I did not consider my family as very political. From what I gathered, Monroe, Louisiana, was noted as a hotbed for Louisiana politics during that era.

On Tuesday, with great anticipation, I dressed up in my best bib and tucker and took myself to the Voter Registrar's office. An elderly woman handed me the requested forms and I began filling them out. When I reached the question: "How would you register: Democrat, Republican, or Independent?" I was stymied. I knew my parents were registered Democrats. I thought maybe Abry was also, although we had never discussed the subject. I really liked the sound of Republican. It had such a nice ring, and I liked the fact that it was the up-and-coming new party. I checked the box, Republican, completed the form, proudly walked back to the desk, and handed the form to the old lady. As she began reading the form, an awful frown came over her face. As she looked up, she asked if my father-in-law was Abry Cahn Sr. I replied that he was. She then wanted to know if I had discussed with my husband the fact that I would be registering as a

Republican. I replied that I had not. She then told me there had never been a registered Republican in the Cahn family, and she was going to do me a favor by not accepting my registration until I discussed it with them.

When Abry came home that evening, and I told him the story, he thought it was the funniest thing he had ever heard. Abry said, "We always have dinner at Honey and Pops on Tuesday, so that will be the perfect opportunity to discuss the matter with Dad." When we arrived, Abry told his dad I had a very important matter to discuss with him. When I finished telling Pops the saga, he thought for a few seconds and said, "I am going to go and talk to Bud." Bud was Pops's brother who lived next door. Pops was gone for a lengthy time. When he finally returned, he said, "We all love you very much, and you tell Miss Jim Martin that whatever you want to do is fine with us. It is important for you to understand that if you register as Republican, you won't be eligible to vote in any of the primaries; you will only be eligible to vote for the President and Vice President." I wasn't sure at the time what any of that really meant, but I thanked him. I asked Pops and Abry to please write a note to Miss Martin to that effect and for both of them to sign the letter. With the letter in hand, I marched back to the Voter Registrar's Office the next day, handed her the letter, took my ballot, and registered as a Republican.

Blessings

Pops, Susan, and Honey.

Susan was born on May 19, 1957, at Highland Hospital. I felt my first twinge of labor pains on Saturday, the day before. Abry phoned my parents in Monroe, and they jumped in the car and arrived at the hospital around 6:00 pm. Abry's parents were there to keep Abry company. Marion and Cerf, Abry's sister and brother-in-law, arrived around 7:00 p.m. with an ice chest full of martinis and hors d'oeuvres for the celebration. My mother was mad as an old wet hen. Susan finally joined the party at 3:00 p.m. on Sunday afternoon. She was a beautiful, perfect little girl. We were blessed; no one could ask for a more perfect child.

Susan attended Southfield Nursery School briefly until one day, the headmaster put her in the wrong car at carpool, and we had no idea where she was until the lady of the house arose from her drunken stupor at 3:00 pm and wanted to know who the extra child was in her home. None of the help knew. She finally contacted someone at the school, and Susan was safely returned. Susan graduated from the University of Texas and married Arthur Ableman of San Antonio on January 16, 1988. Arthur is like one of our very own children. We could not have done better if we had chosen him ourselves.

Tab with grandparents: Honey and Pops.

marAbry Sour Cahn III was born on September 27, 1960. Abry was tied up in a meeting, so I drove myself to the doctor's clinic to get checked out when I felt the first twinges. Dr. Robinson said I was definitely in labor, and I was immediately admitted to the hospital. I phoned the office again and left a message with Mrs. Smith, his secretary, to tell Abry I was at the hospital having a baby. Abry and I had not discussed names if we were having a boy. We both knew his dad made no bones about wanting his grandson to carry on the family name. Abry said it would be fine with him if we could think of an appropriate nickname. Honey, as we called Abry's mom, was a genius with words. She immediately came up with Tab. Everyone was in agreement. By the way, this was about six months before Coke's new drink, "Tab," came on the shelf. I asked her one day how she came up with the name. She said, "I took the 'T' from third and added it to Ab, which was what we called his dad, Abry Jr."

Tab and Pops.

Tab was such a smart little boy that we always had to be two steps ahead of him. He had a mind of his own and knew exactly what he wanted and how to go about getting it. Both children were so responsible that they were each given a car when they were old enough to drive. Tab married Marylyn Haws on May 30, 1992. I could not have picked a more perfect wife for Tab. She is like my very own, and her family has become my extended family—they include me in every holiday celebration. Our grandson, Abry Chandler Cahn, was born on August 23, 1994. He was spared being named a 4th. Fortunately, his parents came up with the beautiful name Chandler for a handsome and perfect young man who has brought us all so much joy. I love you all very much!

Marilyn and Tab.

Reflections

The realization struck shortly after we returned from our honeymoon. Despite dating and corresponding for seven years, we really did not know each other. We were the perfect example of how *"Women are from Venus and Men are from Mars."*

Clothes were a passion of mine. Abry could care less. He was in the habit of having his shoes resoled and wearing them until they came apart. I loved to dance, and Abry had two left feet. Funny that before we married, just being close to each other on the dance floor was the important thing.

A funny incident just came to mind. There was a shoe repair shop on Texas Street, behind Cahn Electric on Milam Street. On this particular day, Abry walked around the corner, planning to have his old shoes resoled. They told him in no uncertain terms that it would not be worth the money and that he should consider walking down the street to the shoe store where they had just received a great selection of new shoes. That evening, Abry came home as a very unhappy person. His new shoes were killing his feet, and he could hardly walk. I told him he needed to take them back and get some that were comfortable. He said, "No, I am going to break them in." There was absolutely no reasoning with him, and this went on for a period of time. One day, Abry came home with the biggest grin on his face. I said, "You look mighty happy today," and he said, "I am. I finally broke my shoes in, and I realized my feet didn't hurt any longer. When I looked down, I realized the shoes had come apart from the sole, and my feet were hanging out. I was so happy I finally broke the shoes in." So much for frugality!

My family was a game-playing family. We played bridge, Bouray[7], poker, dominoes, you name it. On occasion, I could talk Abry into a game of gin rummy. He would rather sit quietly and listen to Mozart. Abry loved the symphony and opera; I loved Elvis and Buddy Holly. Abry bought two season tickets to the symphony and opera, and for years, I went reluctantly. At some point, many years later, I came to the realization that I loved both the symphony and opera. I don't think Abry ever felt the same about either Elvis or Buddy Holly, although we were in New York when the Broadway play *Buddy Holly Story* opened. During the finale, Abry was standing in the aisles, clapping and rocking to the music with me and the rest of the audience.

Abry had a much more sophisticated palette than I, although I think being five years older had a lot to do with that. I had never eaten Chinese or Mexican food until after we married. I think we were both in shock the first time Abry took me to a Chinese restaurant, and I had no clue what to order. Fried chicken, Spaghetti, and meatballs were my comfort food. Marbles Barbecue in Monroe was also one of my favorites.

Abry had taken bridge lessons before we married. One Friday night, I talked him into going to Marie and Forrest Sharp's to play duplicate bridge. We won, although, after the game, Abry said that he worked with numbers all day long and that he had no desire to spend his evenings at a bridge table. We are probably the only married couple with a perfect bridge record. We played once and won once.

Abry was a big Trap shooter and duck hunter, and I had never held a gun. I was looking forward to learning how to shoot. After all, it was something we could do together. My first anniversary present from

---

[7] A variation of Booray, or Bourré

Abry was a 12-gauge Winchester pump with a ventilated rib. My parents were less than impressed; I was thrilled. Abry took me to the gun club and taught me all the safety precautions of shooting. I loved the sport. That fall, I was invited to go on a duck hunt with Abry and the Zadecks to Stuttgart, Arkansas. Abry owned a share in a hunting lease thcrc. Months before the hunt, we went shopping in Eddie Bauer's catalog. Abry ordered me waders and a goose-down hunting coat. I was now ready for the big hunt. I didn't know the difference between a duck and a crane, but fortunately for me, I wasn't a very good shot. We were hunting in the marsh, and the water was well over our knees. We had to wade to the location where we would be hunting. On the way out of the marsh, my boots became stuck in the mud. Abry was already on the bank, so Donald came back to help me. He told me not to try to pull up a foot until he told me. I don't think I was one to follow instructions very well. Being "mother's little helper," I tried to dislodge my foot from the mud too soon; I lurched forward into Donald. He fell backward in the water, and I fell on top of him. The temperature was 17 degrees that day. That was my first and last duck hunt.

During the week, Abry and I would load shotgun shells after dinner several nights. Sunday afternoons were usually spent at the Gun Club shooting trap. Abry and I usually shot in the same squad together. We hired a sitter to stay with Susan so we could both go to the Gun Club. I remember vividly one Sunday when we arrived at the Gun Club, and Abry started saying that he was not going to shoot. I wanted to know why. He said he just really enjoyed watching me. I told him that was a big fat lie. Then the truth came out: he thought it was just too expensive for us to hire a sitter and for both of us to shoot. That was the end of our Gun Club days.

I became pregnant with Tab, and Abry joined a bowling league. I diligently kept score for all the months I was pregnant. I couldn't wait to have the baby so I could start bowling. Abry joined a couples' league organized by the B'nai Brith[8] men's club with the promise that I could join the league as soon as possible.

There was a fancy new bowling shop in town, and the day finally came when I was going to purchase my ball. Abry was giving me the ball for my birthday. I told Abry I did not know what weight ball to buy and that I would appreciate his opinion. Everyone who knew Abry knew he was a practical joker. I just never thought he would pull anything on me. He told me there was a new ball out that was weighted with water, and I should buy the heaviest ball they had because there was a plug in the thumbhole, and they could let out the necessary amount of water to get it to the right weight. I was so naïve I believed him. I pranced into the bowling shop, and the gentleman who owned the shop greeted me and asked if he could be of service. I told him I was there to purchase a bowling ball. He asked me my name and what weight ball I wanted. I went into the spiel about wanting the new ball weighted with water. He was convulsed, and I was mortified.

"There is justice," he said. "I just drilled a ball for a gentleman named Cahn. Is he your father by chance?" When Abry came home that evening, he wanted to know if I had gotten my bowling ball and how it went. I told him I did, and it went great. I said to him, "By the way, the man who waited on me wanted to know if you were my father." When the season was over and it was time to sign up for the fall league, Abry told me I could sign up if I wanted to, but he was going to sit the next one out. After working all day, he was just too tired to bowl in a league. At that point, I realized that other than an occasional evening out for dinner or a movie with friends, there was nothing that Abry and I would be doing together.

My friend and neighbor, Sandra Querbes, had a daughter who was the same age as Susan's. The girls would both be starting kindergarten together. Sandra and I agreed to carpool. One day, she asked me if I

---

[8] B'nai B'rith is a Jewish organization dedicated to improving the quality of life for people around the globe.

played bridge. She said there was a game at Marie and Forrest Sharp's that started at 10:00 AM and ended in time to pick up the girls at Miss Agnew's. This was the beginning of my lifetime playing the game of bridge I loved. When Abry went duck hunting, Sandra and I would take off and go to a tournament. Abry was very supportive of my hobby and my desire to compete. I don't think he ever realized that, if given half a chance, I would have been just as dedicated to shooting, hunting, and bowling with him.

The Search and Find

Abry and I realized that with the new baby, our one-bedroom apartment would be too small. Abry's sister took control of the situation, thinking she knew exactly what we needed. One evening, Abry came home from work with the announcement that we bought a lot on East Ridge and would be building our new home. After dinner, Abry drove me to see what I thought was the ugliest lot I had ever seen. It was a flat pie-shaped piece of property where the two streets, East Ridge and Berkshire, merged. I was told that Abry's uncle could draw up some plans for a nice little modern house with three bedrooms and two bathrooms. I was not a fan of 1950s architecture. While his aunt's and uncle's house was very impressive, I really was not comfortable with modern design. Modern houses were totally unfamiliar to me; they did not have the warm, elegant, homey feel of the traditional design I loved.

Abry and I struggled for several weeks trying to find a happy medium. Eventually, it dawned on Abry that we would never agree on anything related to building a modern home. Several weeks later, when he came home from work, he said the plans for the house were scrapped, and we would no longer be building. He had an opportunity to sell the lot and had accepted the offer. I felt a little guilty that I had not been more cooperative with the plans. However, I was also very relieved. We were now back in search of something acceptable for both of us.

Several weeks went by when Abry called from the office around 10:00 a.m. and wanted to know what I was doing. Seems like his sister Marion had found a house and had talked their dad into going to look at it. They thought the house was perfect for us. Abry said he was on his way to pick me up if it was convenient. The house was the first house to be built in the new Picrmont subdivision on Gilbert near 70th Street. It was around the end of October, and the weather had been bad for about ten days. All the streets were new and had not been paved. The street in front of the house was one big mudhole.

The architect was also a relative of the Cahns. If I thought I did not care for his uncle's modern design, I despised his cousin's. The house was also patterned after Frank Lloyd's 1950s modern architecture. One of the signatures designed by the architect was a brick fireplace that opened into the living room and a small sitting room behind the living room. The little house had a brick front and a clapboard back. The rooms were tiny, and there was no bus service in the new area. This monstrosity was brick and located right in the center of the house. As they all stood there smiling and waiting for my response that I loved the home, Abry said, "Dad and Marion have made a gentleman's agreement with the owners of this house for a very good price of $40,500. All you have to say is yes, and it is ours." Talk about what it feels like to be a rat on a sinking ship. I felt every one of those emotions. I collected my thoughts and, in a little squeaky voice, said, "Honey, I hope y'all will be happy living here because I'm not moving in." Abry and I were now on our own in search of a suitable home.

Our friends Harriette and Imy Marcus were also in the market to buy a home because their apartment was too small. Harriette and I would ride around looking for "For Sale" signs. We mainly looked in the old, established neighborhood of South Highlands around Fairfield Avenue. Most of those homes were too big and out of our price range. The smaller ones needed too much work. One day, Harriette said let's go and look in Broadmoor. It is a new neighborhood that is being developed. Broadmoor had mostly been the cotton fields and was basically still on the outskirts of the cotton fields. We were driving down East Kings Highway when I spotted a "For Sale sign by Owner" on Lynn Avenue. I think I was screeching when I told Harriette, "Turn here." When we passed in front of the house, I fell in love. The month was February, and the flower beds in front of the house were in full bloom with beautiful pansies. The house was a very impressive California ranch, salmon-colored brick with a matching brick wall around the back yard. The house was on a corner lot with the garage and drive facing the side street, Bryan Place. I wrote down the telephone number, and Harriette and I hurried back to my apartment so I could set up an appointment to see the house the next day. The house was owned by Sam and Lessie Love, and the minute I walked in, I knew it was the perfect house. The rooms were a nice size, and the kitchen was enormous. I especially loved the sitting room that had a terrazzo floor and two large windows overlooking the patio and back yard. Sam told Abry he loved the house and really did not want to sell it, which was all his wife's idea. He also said the price was not negotiable. He was asking $40,500. The house needed some work. The colors were very dark, with natural pine woodwork and dark floral wallpaper that was not to my taste, but the house had such good bones that I saw the potential.

Abry wanted his mother, dad, and sister Marion to see the house before he committed. His parents did not have much to say, but his sister had plenty; she was horrified. She said the house was in the low-rent district, in the cotton fields, and that it was on the wrong side of town. She also thought it was overpriced for the location. The house was the largest house in the neighborhood, which was not good. The house was built on two lots; the size was 120 feet by 120 feet. There was no question that the builder had overbuilt the neighborhood. When we parted, I did not like my chances of owning the house. I was surprised, to say the least, when Abry came home that evening and said if I really loved the house on Lynn Street, he would buy it for me. He told me to be sure it was what I wanted because if I said "Yes," he would never move again. He said, "When I go out of this house, it will be feet first."

Abry and I moved into the house on April 1, 1957, and resided there until July 2017. This was a lifetime of mostly 62 happy years.

The only room in the house that was completely furnished was the nursery. Fortunately, there was a chest of drawers in the closet of the master bedroom. We had no headboard. We had a little breakfast room table and chairs, and that was about it.

The only thing we had an abundance of was the dozens of towels in turquoise, pink, and gray colors that went with none of the tiles in any of the bathrooms. I was so happy; none of this bothered me in the least.

We had our work cut out for us because I don't think either one of us had any idea how much work the house really needed. With no furniture in the living room and dining room, we realized that the Loves must have had a dog. There were yellow stains all over the carpet in both rooms. My mother thought she had the perfect fix and she would surprise us. She took herself to the store and bought blue dye and a toothbrush. When she returned home, instead of testing her theory in a small spot, she had very carefully put the blue dye over every spot in both rooms. When Abry walked in and saw the mess, I remember him saying, "What on God's green earth happened in here?" My mother tried to explain that she knew blue and yellow made green, so she thought she had the right combination to fix the yellow spots. My mother said, "I know if I could just get that same dog back, I could get the right color." Abry and I laughed so hard we couldn't stop; she felt so guilty that she replaced the carpet.

In February of 1967, our house burned. We had just installed an alarm system. The kids had left for school about an hour earlier, and I was talking on the telephone when the fire alarm went off, and the phone disconnected. I thought the system had malfunctioned, so I was not concerned. When I walked into the hall entrance to the utility room to turn off the alarm, I saw the flames. I grabbed Yum Yum, the poodle, and my new full-length Mink coat Abry had given me for our tenth wedding anniversary and ran out the back door. I ran across the street and used the Sours telephone to call the fire department. I then called Cahn Electric to tell Abry. Mrs. Smith, Abry's secretary, who was like a member of the family, answered the phone and said, "Nell, he's at the Chamber of Commerce luncheon, and if you want, I can give him a message when he gets back?"

I said, "Tell him our house is on fire." In the meantime, some of the neighbors had gathered with me in the front yard, waiting for the fire department. We heard the sirens and saw the trucks riding up and down East Kings Highway. They were unable to find Lynn Street. Abry and Bob Jackson, Abry's right-hand man at Cahn Electric, arrived in a yellow cab at the same time the Fire Department and TV station did. On the evening news, there was a segment of me walking across the front yard, dragging my fur coat under one arm and carrying my dog under the other, as I watched my home burn.

Both children were hysterical when they came home from school and saw their home practically destroyed. It took some doing to convince them we would not be homeless, just a little inconvenienced for a while.

Everything that did not burn was so saturated with the smell of smoke that all our cloths were unwearable. When I opened the linen closet, the sheets were black with soot. The automatic cut-off to the heating system did not cut off, so smoke and soot were blown throughout the ventilating system. There was massive smoke damage to everything. We collected toothbrushes and a few things that were still usable and moved to Honey and Pops[9] for a few days until we could figure out where we were going to live. I began to see this as a wonderful opportunity to walk away, take the insurance money, sell

---

[9] Abry's mother and father.

the house as is, and buy a nice new house. I was in for a rude awakening. Things don't happen that way in the real world.

We were fortunate in the respect that our across-the-street neighbors were moving and had just listed their home for sale. We were able to convince them to allow us to lease the house if we agreed to allow the relator to show it when necessary.

The next day, Abry had everything completely under control. He took Mr. Tallman, manager, and number one estimator for Werner Company, to the house to assess the damages. Werner Company was the number one commercial construction company in Shreveport at the time. If Werner company was a low bidder on a job, Cahn Electric usually did all the Electrical work. Werner Co. did no residential work. Abry and Mr. Tallman had such a good working relationship that Mr. Tallman agreed to do us a favor and rebuild Lynn Street. I am sure he rued the day he ever agreed to do that. Thinking back, I realize I was a royal pain in Werner's behind. Mr. Tallman thought they would come in, do a slam dunk, and be finished as if they were doing an office building. He had no idea what it was like to work with a woman who was used to always having her way. This was my home, and since I had the wonderful opportunity to rebuild, I wanted the luxury of taking my time to make decisions and possibly make some changes. It was obvious early on that this was not going to happen, and I felt we were at war.

I knew there was trouble when we were standing in the living room one morning, and Mr. Tallman asked me what color I wanted in there. Being very literal, I thought he meant the living room specifically. I said, "Antique White." Later that afternoon, when I returned to check on the progress, the entire interior was painted antique white. I was in tears. Abry said, "No problem, he will paint it over. We are on time and material; pick out the colors you want; all it takes is more time and more money." The house remained all antique white for years. As time went by, I began to like having everything light and bright.

Then there was the issue of the bathroom. There was a new product called Grecian Marble. It was a poured product that looked like marble but was a synthetic substance. I wanted to use this on the counters, in the shower, and in the area above the tub. Mr. Tallman was against the idea. He felt tile was proven, and he knew nothing about Grecian Marble. One day, Mr. Tallman told Abry, "I think your wife is mad at me." Abry said, "Why would you say that?" Mr.Tallman said, "She wants to use that Grecian Marble in the bathroom." Abry said, "What did you tell her?" Mr.Tallman said, "I told her no." Abry said, "She is mad; no one has ever told her no." Abry and Mr. Tallman finally agreed we could use Grecian Marble on everything except around the tub because he was afraid of a moisture problem, and we would use tile there. Abry told me that if I didn't like the tile around the tub, it could always be ripped out. When the bathroom was finished, it was beautiful. When Mr. Tallman said, "Now, doesn't the tub look wonderful also with the tile? I said, "Rip it out." There was a stunned silence. No one said a word until I said, "Honey, you promised." Abry said, "Rip it out because I will never hear the end of this, and to do it now is the cheapest thing we can do."

A number of years later, when the casinos opened, I was very lucky to hit a large jackpot. I decided to take the money and remodel the kitchen, which was definitely overdue. Granite had been in vogue for a number of years, and we were still sporting Formica. It was definitely time for a change. I selected the granite and picked out a very expensive Shumaker wallpaper that I was in love with. Mimi and Pawpaw were coming for Thanksgiving, and we were in a time crunch to finish before they arrived.

We picked them up at the airport and entered the house through the garage into the newly re-done kitchen. When I saw my mother's face, I knew something was definitely wrong. I said, "Well, do you just love it?" She was very slow to answer, but when she finally did, it was definitely not what I expected to hear; she said, "It is upside down."

"What is upside down, I asked?"

"The wallpaper, they hung it upside down."

"I asked her why she would say that."

"Well," she said, "their little feet are going toward the ceiling."

"What feet?" I spoke.

"The feet on the little birds."

"Oh my God! Birds??? I thought they were flowers!"

After a closer look, I saw they were definitely birds, and their feet were pointed toward the ceiling.

You just can't make this up!

The Maxim Machine Guns

Re: Spandau MG 08 Serial # 9336

Erfurt MG 08/15 Serial # 8484

My husband, along with his dad and uncle Henry Cahn, owned Cahn Electric Co. at 708 Milam Street. In 1956, they were approached by the USO with a request to use their show window facing Milam Street for a display for the Armistice Day parade on November 11. The display consisted of two machine guns manned by two mannequins dressed in soldier uniforms and a couple of mannequins dressed in nurses' uniforms. The display remained at the store for weeks after the parade was over. My husband kept calling the USO office, trying to get someone to come and dismantle the display and remove it. They never returned his calls. Much to his dismay, one day, he found out that the USO office had closed, and everyone had left town. Not knowing what to do with the two machine guns, Abry decided the best thing would be to store them on the third floor of the building until further notice.

Fast forward to 1968: Our son Tab loved to go with his dad on the weekends when he went to the office. There were lots of nooks and crannies on the upper floors of the old Milam Street building, which he loved to explore. One Sunday, Tab came across the two machine guns tucked away on the third floor on an upper shelf almost to the ceiling. In 1968, everyone was required to register firearms. Tab was so excited when he found the guns because he had heard us talk about

97

the USO leaving them at the store after the parade. He could not wait to tell his dad that he found them. My husband, who followed the law to a fault, immediately phoned to register the guns. When told that he was not required to register most handguns, he replied that they were not most handguns. When he told the person he was talking about two machine guns, the agent became a lot more attentive. As Abry told the story, he had barely hung up the phone before two plain-clothed Federal agents were standing in his office on Milam Street. After due process, the guns were finally registered to Abry Cahn Jr with a list of instructions as to his responsibility for owning machine guns. He was never to give the guns away or sell the guns. This did not sound good. We would have to bury Abry with the guns.

Again, fast forward to 1973: Tab was going to junior high school at First Baptist School and working on a war project for his social studies class. He asked his dad for some suggestions, and Abry said if we were able to get approval from the school, how would you like to make a display with the two machine guns? The school gave the approval, and the display was not only used for Tab's class project; it ended up being a display the entire school was able to enjoy as an educational project for all the students. Tab received an A++ for his project.

That same year, Cahn Electric was moving from 708 Milam Street to their new building at 2154 Midway. They had outgrown the Milam Street facility. Unfortunately, there was no place for the machine guns on Midway. Much to Tab's excitement, after the display at First Baptist closed, we brought the guns to our home at 120 Lynn Avenue. They remained there until July of 2017.

Our house: 120 Lyn Street, Shreveport, Louisiana.

A Period of Adjustments

My mother always said, "Life was simply a period of adjustments." It was 1965; Susan was eight years old, and Tab was five. Pawpaw came home one evening and told Mimi the company he worked for had been sold to XOM, and he was being transferred to New Orleans to run the office. Mimi was not happy. It took a lot of convincing from everyone that this would be the beginning of a great new adventure for not just them but for all of us.

Susan and Mardi Gras.

Tab attending Mardi Gras, New Orleans.

We had a lot of "firsts" that year; the kids' first Mardi Gras was definitely the most exciting. Mimi and Pawpaw bought a townhouse on St. Charles Avenue on the parade route where the Rex parade turned around on Mardi Gras Day. We visited for the entire week of Mardi Gras, and what a time we all had. Abry had made each of the kids a special contraption: a big brown paper sack attached to a long broom handle with signs that read, "Throw Me Something, Mister." We set up ladders on the neutral ground so the children could have a good view of the parade. Pawpaw held Susan, and Abry held Tab. When the float stopped, the revelers dumped armfuls of beads and Doubloons into their sacks, and the kids thought it was the most exciting thing that had ever happened. When it was time to head back to Shreveport, they loaded their sacks of Mardi Gras treasures into the car, anxious to show their friends all their loot and already talking about returning next year.

The children were becoming more involved with their activities, such as Susan with Brownie Scouts, dancing lessons, and singing lessons. Abry had taken over the chore of Cub Scout leader for Tab and his group. Abry was also very busy teaching him gun safety to make sure he would be ready for their first hunting expedition. Also, in the spring, Tab will start playing little league baseball. Susan had been chosen as one of the cheerleaders, and I volunteered as a chaperone on the trips out of town. Abry and I both chaperoned the socials for the school until the kids begged us to give it up; we were spoiling their fun.

Life was good, and the Cahn family owned a camp on Cross Lake. On weekends, weather permitting, we would head for the lake to ride in the boat, fish off the dock, and a Weenie roast. One weekend, Mimi and Pawpaw were in town. We packed our picnic basket and headed for the camp. Honey, Pops, Pawpaw, and Tab were on the dock getting ready to fish when Tab slipped and fell into the lake. Fortunately, Pawpaw saw it and jumped in fully dressed to rescue him. I become frightened all over again every time I think about the incident. Susan and Tab had become so busy that it was impossible to get everyone together for outings at the lake. Several years went by. Abry came home one evening and said the family had made the decision to sell the camp. It had not been used in years, and there was no sense in keeping it. We all knew this was the truth, but I think everyone still felt bad. I guess we just assumed it would always be there, just in case we want to go back someday. Letting go is always a hard thing to do.

Susan spent many of her summers at camp. Tab went once, and when it was time to fill out the applications for the next year, he said, "Mom... Dad... I went once and did not complain; I'm not going back again; it is not for me." He handled this in such a mature manner that there was no argument we could possibly come up with, so we simply said OK.

Abry and I had given up on taking any major trips out of the country for a while. It was just too difficult with all the kids' activities.

In 1967, after the Six-Day War, the Rabbi organized a trip to Israel that was sponsored by the Shreveport Jewish Federation. I couldn't remember when I had seen Abry so excited; l hated to rain on his parade. The children were small and I did not feel we should both leave them on a trip that could involve possible danger. Clifford Bayer, Abry's childhood friend, was anxious to go, and I insisted that Abry go as well. Clifford would be a great traveling companion. When Abry returned, he said it was one of the most rewarding experiences of his life. He was so appreciative that I had insisted and was sorry that I had not gone with him. Looking back, even if I had known everything would go according to plan, I am not sure I would have agreed to take the trip at that time.

Things were beginning to heat up with integration. Both Susan and Tab were enrolled at Arthur Circle Elementary School. The school was so convenient that it was within walking distance from our house on Lynn Street. They loved their teachers and all their friends and school activities. We began hearing rumblings that things were going to change. There would be bussing, and our children might not be allowed to continue at Arthur Circle School. John Golson, a friend of ours and Susan's teacher, called Abry and told him he would like to come over that evening as there was something he wanted to discuss. When John arrived, he did not pull any punches. The first thing he said when he walked in the door was, I'm leaving Arthur Circle School at the end of the month. I will be Head Master at First Baptist Church school. I would not be here if I did not think it was really important that y'all should consider enrolling Susan and Tab before they fill their quota. John said that members of the church had first priority. Abry said, "Hell, tell them we will join the church." John felt that wasn't going to be necessary if we got our application in immediately. I think Abry and I both realized that this was possibly one of the most important decisions regarding our children's upbringing we had ever faced. After much deliberation and agreement from Susan and Tab, it was farewell to Arthur Circle.

First Baptist Church School... here we come.

Life rocked along with trips to New Orleans with Susan and Tab. Abry was president of NECA (National Electrical Contractors) for three years. We went to the national conventions in Miami, Toronto, and Hawaii during his time as president. These were all great trips. The year Susan turned sixteen and became eligible for her driver's license, we decided the safest way to get around her being in a car on New Year's Eve would be to take a family cruise. All went pretty well until I accidentally left all the cruise ship tickets on the plane in Dallas. I didn't realize my mistake until we arrived in Miami and Abry asked me about the tickets for the cruise – I panicked. Abry went to check with American Airlines. When he returned, he said, "There is good news and bad news. The good news is they found the tickets. The bad news is the plane is en route to Bangor, Maine." Hopefully, they will have them back in Miami tomorrow before we board the ship at 4:00 pm. Around 2:00 pm, as we were frantically trying to figure out what to do next, the front desk called to let us know a taxi driver was in the lobby with some tickets.

All's well that ends well.

Pawpaw, Susan, Mimi, and Tab.

Birthday Memories

This morning, when I turned the page of my date book and saw August 1, I suddenly felt an emotion when I realized it was once again my birthday month. I immediately had a flashback to my 16th birthday. My mother had made an appointment for us to meet with Mr. Paul, the baker, and a true artist, to select my birthday cake. I had no idea my parents were planning a surprise party for me with all of my friends. I thought it would just be family as usual, which was pretty much a party within itself. I had never met Mr. Paul before, and I will never forget him. He had a huge smile and the kindest face filled with love I had ever seen, and I could tell he absolutely loved what he was doing. He said, "Nell, I understand you and your mother are here to select a cake for your very special birthday, and I have been chosen to make you the most beautiful cake you will always remember." He took me into a room with a display of more decorated cakes than I could ever imagine. I could have selected any one of them because they were all beautiful, but none of them were the perfect ones. After a few minutes, Mr. Paul asked me if any of the cakes had spoken to me and if I had made a decision. I told him I really did not see the special one, and he asked me what that would be like. I told Mr. Paul I had always dreamed of a cake with little blue birds on it. He got so excited and told me that was exactly what I would have. As I write this story, I try to recall the party, what I wore, and the gifts my parents gave me. To tell you the truth, I can't remember anything about any of that. The only thing I can remember is the excitement and joy I felt when they brought my magnificent birthday cake decorated with the little blue birds to the table and lovingly placed it in front of me.

After Abry and I married, with his birthday being on August 10th and mine on the 12th, we celebrated both on the 11th. Each year, Abry would ask if I wanted to do something special for my birthday, and I would tell him that celebrating our birthdays together was what I wanted. However, I would take him up on his offer for my 50th birthday, so he should start saving up. Every year after that, he wanted to know what I wanted to do on my 50th, and I told him I'd let him know closer to the time. On my 49th birthday, I finally told him I wanted to spend a weekend in Paris in a suite at the Ritz Hotel. It was all I had ever dreamed of. Nothing I could write would ever do that weekend justice. When the bellman opened the door, and I stepped into the living room, I almost fainted. The walls were buttercup yellow, and the drapes were emerald green Peau De Soie[10]. I felt like royalty, a dream come true. We packed more into those three days than you can imagine. I always heard that you had not really lived until you had eaten a hot dog from a cart on the Champs-Élysées. Abry said, "With all the fabulous restaurants in Paris, I can't believe you would waste a meal doing that, but your wish is my command. Hot dogs it is." To this day, I remember it being the most delicious hot dog I have ever eaten, and I will always cherish the memory.

We celebrated my 40th birthday in New Orleans with my parents, Abry, Susan, and Tab. Abry told me I could select any restaurant I wanted. My pick was a fairly new restaurant across the river, La Ruth's. We dressed to the nines for the special occasion. The restaurant was charming, and the dinner was divine. The menu had several unusual choices, one of which I decided to order as one of my sides: broiled bananas. The dish really sounded yummy. Unfortunately, at the time, I did not realize I would end up wearing them. I thought things were going quite well until the waiter leaned

---

[10] A smooth, finely ribbed satin fabric of silk or rayon.

over, and the dish of bananas slid off the tray into my hair and all down the back of my new dress. I wish I could have taken a photo of the look of horror on everyone's face. What a mess. On my lucky day, though, I wasn't hurt; dinner was free, the restaurant bought me a new dress, and everyone had a good time.

Abry had been in the nursing home for several years, and a birthday celebration for my 80th birthday was the last thing I wanted. Susan and Arthur, as well as Marylyn and Tab, insisted on having a party for me with close friends and family. They contacted John Cariere, my dear friend and the best caterer I have ever known, to prepare a lavish and delicious buffet. They decorated the Lynn St. house, and when they finished, it looked like a fairyland. I am truly blessed with the most loving and caring family anyone could possibly have. This year, I will turn 87, a new beginning.

Travels

Abry and I were very fortunate to be able to take advantage of numerous traveling opportunities while we were young. We started our first-anniversary celebration with a cruise to the Caribbean with my cousin Marilyn Rolnick and her husband, Maury. The ship was from the Italian Costa line, and the name, the Franca C, was very small with only one engine. We were having a wonderful time and everything went well until the engine went out. The mechanic on the ship was unable to remedy the problem, so we were helplessly adrift until they could locate someone experienced to work on the engine. I remember the crew fishing off the back of the ship. When I asked one of them what he expected to catch, he said, "Sharks, of course." At this point, I thought the best thing I could do would be to return to the cabin and take a nap.

The two main islands we visited were San Juan and St. Thomas. St. Thomas is known for its beautiful jewelry and has some of the finest jewelry stores in the world. Abry bought me a beautiful gold and diamond cocktail ring at H. Stearns, which I am still enjoying.

Several years passed when Abry came home one day and asked if I would like to go to Monte Carlo and the French Riviera. The appliance section of Cahn Electric was a distributor of GE built-ins. From the late 1950s until the early 1990s, GE's way of rewarding its top producers was by giving away fabulous vacations for their outstanding performance. For many decades, Cahn Electric was the recipient of these fabulous vacations.

In September of 1959, Susan was two years old. We took her to Monroe to stay with Mimi and Pawpaw, and off to the French Riviera we went.

The tour was leaving from New York, and I had never been to the big city. Honey and Pops thought it would be fun to come with us to New York several days before our departure and give us a big sendoff. Bill Pfeifer, Honey's nephew, had just completed the restoration of one of the first Carriage houses in the Bronx for his home, which was beautiful. The house was featured in the Sunday section of the *New York Times* the day before we arrived. I felt very proud to be part of this amazing family. My first ride on a subway to see Cousin Bill's carriage house was a first I'll never forget. It was raining like "hell." I had on a new, very expensive navy crepe suit, and by the time we arrived at Bill's, the suit was soaking wet and had started to shrink. To say the least, I was an absolute mess. I remember thinking that if my mother had been here, she would have laughed and said, "Don't you think that with all their money, they could afford to take a limo?" We had a marvelous time with Bill, and we promised to keep in touch and make plans to get together again soon.

We arrived in Nice, France, and boarded a bus that took us to the Carlton Hotel in Cannes, France. The hotel looked like a palace, and it was so elegant. Our room overlooked the Mediterranean, and Abry could not wait to run to the window to look at the topless bathing beauties we had read so much about.

Fortunately, Abry had one wonderful evening before he came down with a travel bug and was out of commission for the next two days. He insisted it was very important for him that I take advantage of all the tours so I could tell him everything he was missing. On the third day, he said he thought he was feeling well enough to join the group for lunch. We were going to a very famous restaurant that featured a special soup. He said that soup sounded like just what the doctor ordered.

The soup was "Bouillabaisse." The clear broth was ladled into Abry's bowl, and he picked up his soup spoon, ready to dig in when the waiter said, "No, no, monsieur." The waiter then spooned in some clams, shrimp, green herbs, and the finishing touch—a whole fish with head and eyes staring up out of the bowl. The minute the fish hit the bowl, Abry turned green and ran to the door, saying, "Enjoy your lunch, folks. Sorry, I have to leave." When we finished eating, one of the men at the table asked for the check. The waiter said, "The gentleman who left took care of the check and said to tell everyone he hoped they enjoyed the meal. He said he felt so miserable that he was going to buy everyone lunch so he could be completely miserable. So much for Bouillabaisse." Fortunately, Abry recovered in time to board the bus to Monte Carlo and our stay at the Hotel de Paris. We visited the village of Eze and dined at the famous restaurant, La Taverne d'Antan à Eze, which was extraordinaire. Even with Abry's little episode, the trip was truly amazing.

The following year, our travels took us to Madrid and Costa del Sol. During that trip, we connected with a couple from Alexandria, Louisiana, Sammy and Phyllis Dunbar. Sammy loved researching the places we visited and always had recommendations for the best restaurants and hot spots. One of our favorite haunts in Costa del Sol was a small piano bar with an amazing pianist who had a great voice. By the end of the vacation, Sammy and Abry were so enthralled that they invited him to come to the States for a visit.

Nell, Abry, Sammy, and Phyllis Dunbar.

A trip to Portugal, Tangier, and Turkey was scheduled for the next year. In Estoril, Portugal, there was a mix-up with the transportation to the airport for our return. The day before our departure, when the GE officials checked with the bus company, there was no record of any reservations made for our transportation, and the company had no buses available. Somehow, through another company, they managed to locate 15 black stretch limousines ready for service. As they were loading the luggage into the limos, six buses arrived in front of the hotel, creating a horrific traffic jam. It seemed like an eternity, but it only took about thirty minutes before the luggage was loaded onto the buses, the limos were sent away, and we were on our way to the airport on time.

We were never privy to what caused the mix-up, so all I have to say is, "All's well, and that ends well."

Yugoslavia was a vacation that Abry and I would have never chosen on our own. The opportunity was just too good to pass up, and the Dunbars would also be going, so we knew we would have a great time no matter what. Split was a very poor and dreary place, but when we arrived in Dubrovnik, it looked like paradise. Our hotel was modern and beautiful, overlooking the most stunning body of water, the Adriatic Sea. This was a complete about-face from the impoverished city of Split. We toured Old Town, which was amazing. The synagogue in Dubrovnik is the oldest Sephardic synagogue in the world, said to have been established in 1352. Visiting the synagogue was number one on Abry's to-do list. Unfortunately, it was under repair when we were there and closed to visitors. Our alternate plan was a tour of the rural area up the mountain.

Our tour guide gave a little lecture on things not to do. Foremost was not drinking or eating milk products because the goat milk was not pasteurized. He explained very clearly that there would be men with goat carts selling ice cream, which would be very tempting, but do not be tempted. I have no idea where Abry Cahn was during this lecture—*maybe taking a little nap?* The bus stopped outside of a small village with an outdoor market. The ladies all shopped around, enjoying the handmade wares. When we started back to the bus, I saw Abry down the road with a huge ice cream cone up to his mouth. I screamed, but it was too late. The damage was done. We boarded the bus and headed back to the hotel. About halfway down the mountain, Abry told the bus driver he needed to find a restroom quickly; the bus driver told Abry it was impossible. Abry said, "You stop the bus, and I have to get out now!" A miracle happened; the driver found a place he could stop, and somehow, Abry found a bush. He eventually returned to the bus. We managed to get him back to the hotel and a doctor before all "Hell" broke loose again. Think he will ever learn?

As the '90s approached, the travel life as we knew it with GE was beginning to change. One of the last trips we were privy to was what they called "The Millionaire Dream Yachting Vacation." The old saying, "If it is too good to be true, it probably is," came home to roost. GE offered a trip to the nine top proprietors in the region—the criteria for the trip sales in excess of 1 million dollars. We were flown to Nassau and taken to the Nassau Yacht Club for the first night of our fabulous vacation. We dined on broiled Lobster and Chateaubriand. The evening was amazing.

The next morning, we met for a champagne brunch and drawing for our yacht. Abry and I would be sailing on yacht three. After brunch, we all went to the dock to board our respective vessels. The captain of the yacht one looked so elegant, wearing a white blazer with navy slacks. The first yacht departed, and yacht two arrived at the dock. The captain and crew were immaculate; the captain, wearing a navy blazer with white slacks, was impressive, and I could not wait to see what we could have in store. The three couples boarded yacht two and quickly departed, making room for yacht three: The Cotton Queen.

I had run to the restroom, and when I returned to the dock, I saw this slob of a man standing at the entrance of our yacht. He was wearing a dirty T-shirt, his belly button was hanging out from under the shirt, and a dirty dish towel was dangling over his belt. His first mate was a large gal who looked like Daisy Mae. He was wearing cut-off jeans shorts, and I was sick. I sent Abry to find out what the devil was going on.

The original captain of our yacht had taken off with all the food money, and this was his temporary replacement. Abry told me the saga, and I was ready to jump ship. Abry said, "Honey, be a sport. This will be a great adventure." I should have been the voice of my conviction, but I wasn't. When they revved up the engines, black smoke came out. We were assured everything would be fine once we were in open waters. The bar was stocked with the finest, but when they started mixing drinks, we had no trouble figuring out there was no ice. No problem, they said, we will radio one of the other yachts and have them send some over. The yacht pulled up, and here came the bucket of ice on a gaffing pole. Everyone was happy with the exception of me. I did not drink alcohol, and my Coke did very little to put me into a festive mood.

It began to rain, and we needed to lower the shades to keep the rain off the deck. One small problem: the black smoke started backing up into the closed deck, making breathing difficult. Thinking it was time to retreat to my cabin, I headed downstairs. Our cabin shared a bathroom with the other small cabin. I made the decision to make a pit stop along the way. When I tried to flush the john, it would not flush because the electrical system was not functioning. The thought crossed my mind that we were in big trouble. Around 5:00 pm, we were in a position to dock at the first port, "Hog Island." The first two yachts were already in place, and their crew had decorated them with streamers of flags with their yacht's colors flowing in the breeze. It was dusk, and it was a beautiful sight when the lights came on. Now, it was our turn to dock. As they plugged us into the dock power, there was a terrible sound, and everything was in total darkness. Our yacht had shorted out all the power on the dock and most of the island. The other two yachts had generators and were up and running immediately. I think our yacht was what is known as "Being dead in the water."

The one good thing that happened was that the rain stopped, and we were able to get off the yacht and stretch. There was a large café not too far from the dock. We walked there with the other two couples and crew. Much to Abry's delight, there were a couple of pool tables and a jukebox. Abry got himself a beer and a coke for me and went to join the guys playing pool. The captain made an announcement that there was a casino and a good restaurant on the other side of the island if anyone was interested. Everyone else said they were staying put, but I convinced Abry that it would be a welcome change. The captain said he had a couple of big flashlights if we wanted to go back to the yacht and try to freshen up a bit before we left. This seemed like a great idea. I went back to the cabin and realized my hair was a mess. During that era, wiglets were a very popular thing. I had just gotten a curly new wiglet for the trip. I plopped the wiglet on my head and, feeling pretty chipper, returned to collect Abry for our adventure.

The captain was waiting in the car as Abry and I strolled out of the café. Oh my God. The car was a dilapidated green 1940s DeSoto. I was beginning to have second thoughts when the captain said, "Welcome aboard." It was too late to back out, so off we went.

We had been driving for about ten minutes when the car made a few odd noises and came to a standstill. The engine was dead as a doornail, and we were in the middle of nowhere. Abry, being the gentleman, said, "I will be happy to walk back to the café and get us some help. I said, "No way, wasn't a chance in "Hell" he was leaving me in the middle of that God-forsaken place alone with the captain. The captain said, "No, it is my place. I will walk back." Thinking to myself, he probably wouldn't come back, I said, "Nothing doing; we will all walk back together," and that is exactly what we did.

When we dragged ourselves back into the café, everyone stared at us as if they were watching a horror show. My wiglet was straggling in my face, my shoes were a muddy mess, and we all looked like something the cat had dragged in. Surprisingly, it was almost a welcome relief to return to our dark yacht, banked next to the damp, smelly concrete wall.

There were no other sleeping accommodations on the island, so we were basically stuck in our hot cabin. Around 2 in the morning, I could not stand it any longer, so I decided to go to the top deck to cool it off. When I started down the ladder of my bunk, Abry woke up and wanted to know where I was going. He said, "Just wait a minute. I'll get dressed, and I'm going with you. I don't want you to go alone." I really couldn't imagine what kind of problem he anticipated until we arrived. When we got to the top deck, there was the captain lying on his back on a chaise lounge, necked as a jaybird snoring away. That was the last straw. I started to cry and was inconsolable.

The next morning, Abry told me to pack up that we were going back to Nassau. GE had a suite for us at the Emerald Isle Hotel for the weekend and already had me booked into the spa with a complimentary hair appointment. What a welcomed relief! While on the trip, Abry had taken amazing photographs. Looking back at the pictures, you would think this was the most unbelievable vacation anyone had ever taken. Little did they know.

About a year later, I was reading the *Wall Street Journal* and came across the article that the charter yacht, "The Cotton Queen," sank in the Caribbean. I'm not sure I remember correctly, but I think it read that everyone on board drowned. One thing that I do know is that timing is everything in life; you can't make it up.

Where There's a Will, There's a Way

Growing up, and even now, my biggest problem has always been that it never occurs to me that I can't do anything and everything I want to. This attitude dates back to when I thought I could slide down the seesaw backward, resulting in 144 splinters being plucked out of my behind. That was quite a learning experience.

When Abry and I moved into the Lynn Street house, we were living on a shoestring with very little money to spend on décor. This was one of the big reasons I decided to revisit painting. I knew how to stretch a large canvas, and paint was cheap. It took a number of years, but I was finally able to cover the bare walls at a minimum cost, and the result was very satisfying. I wasn't nearly as successful with my knitting attempt.

My friend Harriette Marcus had opened a knit shop. I had little patience for knitting. Most of my friends thought it was therapeutic, and I wanted to learn because silk ribbon knit sweaters and dresses had become very fashionable and were very expensive to buy, readymade. I had seen an emerald green silk ribbon knit sweater trimmed with black Angora thread that I was dying for. I had no interest in learning how to knit with wool thread, which was the common practice, just to have something to do in my spare time, of which I had little. I wanted to start with the silk ribbon so I would have something to show for my efforts. Harriette had no success in trying to convince me that this probably was not a good idea and that I should have a practice run with basic material. I said, "Look, Harriett, knitting is knitting. Just sell me the silk ribbon and the correct size needles, and give me a couple of lessons." The ribbon was sold by the skein, and it never occurred to me to ask the price. Much to my chagrin, it was very expensive – $50 a skein, even with a family discount. I also didn't know that it was very difficult to work with because it had no give, making it impossible to rip out when you made a mistake. In fact, you can't rip out a ribbon because it falls apart and is not reusable.

This project took place after I had broken my ankle when the horse fell with me on our family vacation in Colorado. I thought it would keep me occupied. I would sit on the couch in the sunroom and basically did more ripping out than I did knitting. I would have piles of emerald green, useless ribbon on the floor that I didn't want Abry to see. Whenever I heard Abry coming in the back door, I would kick the pile of ribbon under the couch.

Visiting the sick was very popular in the old days. One evening during that time, Abry's cousin Lester Haas and his beautiful wife Niki came to pay a visit. Niki sat on the couch next to me, and when she stood to leave, the heel of her shoe got tangled up in a piece of the green ribbon I had kicked under the couch. As she began to walk to the door, the whole pile of stuff came dragging out behind her. Abry said, "What the hell?" Lester and Niki were in complete shock, and all I could do was laugh. Everyone was looking at me as if I was crazy, and I couldn't stop laughing. Abry made a feeble attempt to explain that I was trying to learn how to knit. After Lester untangled the mess from the heel of her shoe, Niki put on her gloves and hat and mumbled something to the effect that she hoped I had a speedy recovery and that she would bring me some magazines I might enjoy so I could give up knitting.

Nothing is Forever

Times were changing; Mimi and Pawpaw were living the good life in New Orleans, and we all enjoyed spending as much time there with them as possible. We loved Mardi Gras and were anxious to try to make that one of our yearly family get-togethers.

Buzz Harper with his two dogs.

Buzz Harper and Les Wisinger had returned to New Orleans and opened Harper's Antiques. Buzz had purchased Ella Brennan's house on Prytania Street and was in the throes of restoring the house when Mimi was introduced to them. Buzz and Les, avid bridge players, were ready to play at any given moment.

Les was a fabulous decorator, and the house and gardens looked like a million dollars in a very short period of time. They frequently entertained, and Mimi and Pawpaw were often included. One of the highlights of my visits was also being the recipient of their fabulous hospitality for dinner and bridge on many occasions. Buz was a wonderful pianist, and some evenings included chamber music or a quartet from the New Orleans Symphony Orchestra for entertainment.

During that period, I was on the bridge circuit, playing at least one major tournament a month and enjoying a successful run. Abry was busy with business, and weekends were filled with hunting, fishing, and playing Pool. Tab was no longer living at home, but Susan returned after graduating from UT and lived with us until she and Arthur married in 1988.

Susan, Abry, and I took a number of trips together during that time. One of our favorites was going to London with Bill Pfeifer when he went to buy antiques for his shop on Madison Avenue in New York. Every summer, Bill took an apartment at the Grosvenor House for a month. On several occasions, Abry, Susan, and I were fortunate enough to be able to join him for a week of his stay. We hit all the shops and booths on Portobello Road every day, and occasionally, in the evenings, we went to the theater. The London theater was fabulous, and one trip in particular stands out in my memories. "Cats" had only been open for about a week, and Bill was able to get us all tickets. The musical was the most spectacular thing I had ever seen.

Peggy Funt, daughter of Allen Funt and host of Candid Camera, was a business associate and Bill's friend. We were invited to her apartment on occasion to shop her wares. It was always fun meeting other dealers, hearing about the exciting treasures they had purchased, and figuring out the hot items everyone was searching for that season.

On May 14, 1999, Susan, Arthur, Abry, and I embarked on a Mediterranean voyage. It was the maiden voyage of the Celebrity ship Century. A day prior to boarding the ship, we were informed that our embarkation had been changed. We had to transfer ourselves and our luggage from Venice to Savona by train, which was no easy task at best. We had no sooner gotten settled when the conductor announced the train had a problem and we would have to transfer to another train on an upper track. You must understand this was before any of the luggage had wheels. I have no idea how they did it, but Susan, Abry, and Arthur managed to get the luggage to the upper track and onto the train; I was useless. The ship was beautiful, and we had no trouble adjusting to life aboard. The captain of the ship was from Greece, and we had a royal welcome into the Athens port, which had flags and music, a site to behold.

On May 19, we celebrated Susan's birthday on board. We informed the kitchen that we wanted to surprise her with a birthday cake. They brought the cake to the table and sang Happy Birthday. They took the cake away and brought a dessert menu. Our daughter said, "No, we want my cake and ice cream." We were told the cake was made of plastic and not consumption. The maitre'd had bowed graciously when we entered the dining room and informed us that he was at our service. Strangely enough, he was nowhere to be found when he needed to be. As each day went by, we heard numerous stories similar to ours that had taken place in the dining room.

June 14, 2006, Star Princess

Susan, Arthur, Marylyn, Chandler, and Abry's cousin Bill Pfeifer joined Abry and me onboard the Star Princess to tour Scandinavia and Russia. The trip was amazing, but the only thing that made it less than perfect was that Tab was unable to join us. This trip celebrated our 50th wedding anniversary. We flew into Copenhagen, took the canal cruise, saw the Little Mermaid, toured Tivoli gardens, and enjoyed the beauty of the city.

Chandler was intrigued by Russia and the fact that Grandpa Kaplan and Grandma were born in Russia and that Grandpa had marched in the Russian army for 3 cents a day. There were numerous vendors on the street selling their wares, and Chandler wanted to buy every army helmet or hat he saw. Abry had to put his foot down when Chandler tried to insist that he needed to buy a gas mask to take home.

May 24, 2008, Liberty of the Seas

Sussan, Arthur, Marylyn, Tab, and Chandler joined Abry and me on the Liberty of the Seas, touring the Eastern Caribbean. It was on this trip that, several nights before our return, Abry had a problem with a rapid heartbeat. We got him to the infirmary, where they told us that if they could not get the rhythm under control, we would have to put him in a hospital in the next port, which was a very small town in Mexico. This had us all freaked out. Fortunately, things worked out, and we made it home ok.

June 9, 2012, Phone call notifying me of Bill Pfeifer's death.

Abry was co-executor of Bill's estate. If he was unable to serve, the responsibility was mine. Bill had also left all the contents of his estate to Abry and me. The week prior, Abry was diagnosed with dementia, so it fell my lot to take his place.

Dining

D ining has always been a big thing with my family, and as far back as I can remember, the family always sat down at 6:00 pm for dinner. When traveling, we always made a big deal about researching the best restaurants, which weren't necessarily the most expensive but always excellent. Some of my fondest memories aren't necessarily about the food.

In 1975, Susan was doing an internship in New York. Abry, Tab, and I went up to spend the last weekend with her. The kids had never been to New York, so Abry and I thought this would be a great opportunity to see the city. Abry, Tab, and I were staying at Abry's cousin Bill Pfeifer's timeshare off 53rd and Madison Ave.

Bill had made reservations for all of us as his guests for dinner at the Rainbow Room. Bill was very generous about some things but very frugal about others. We collected Susan in a taxi and met Bill at the Rainbow Room. It was truly an enchanted evening. The food, music, and service were unbelievable, and the decor reminded me of those in a grand palace in Europe. We finished around 10:45, and when we went downstairs to leave, it was pouring cats and dogs. There wasn't a taxi to be seen in the area. There were some limousines lined up waiting for the shows to be over. Abry rolled up his pants and waded over to one. He made a deal for $50 to take us back to Bill's. Relief was all I could feel, and then Bill said, "Absolutely not, that is highway robbery. We will find some other means." By then, the rain had started to subside, and the water had drained off the streets. It was almost midnight by then. Bill said, "No problem, the bus stop is only a block away, and we have it made now." We all marched to the bus stop, and shortly it arrived. Bill paid for our seats, and we all breathed a sigh of relief. I think we all looked around the bus at the same time and noticed every seat was filled with men wearing black tuxedos. Bill looked up and said in his high, squeaky voice, "Oh, my God! I paid $600 for dinner at the Rainbow Room, and we are riding the fucking bus home with the waiters."

Several nights later, we dined at a restaurant that had been recommended to us, Little Italy. The restaurant was very casual, with long picnic benches for seats, family style, no small tables, and everyone was seated together in a long row. We ordered some Chianti and got in the swing of things, meeting some of the folks we were seated next to, playing geography as to where they were from, etc., when all of a sudden, I heard someone say, "Look out, when I looked up, I saw a buxom waiter with a huge tray of pasta with red sauce over his head spiraling towards our table. The pasta and sauce flew off the tray and exploded on the table and into the wine glasses. We were all drenched in red sauce, noodles, and Chianti. When I realized everyone was O K, I started to laugh and couldn't stop. No one else shared my sense of humor. Somehow, we managed to get ourselves together and out of the restaurant. We flagged a taxi, and once inside, I told Susan to put on my London Fog coat. I had checked at the door and noticed that the coat was the only piece of clothing that wasn't drenched. I told her to take off her clothes under the coat, and I would take them to the cleaners. She was quite upset, as she still had several days of her seminar and was running low on clean clothes. Somehow, she managed to do this by the time the cab arrived at her dormitory. All's well that ends well.

Thanks to being in a big city with a 24-hour dry cleaning service.

My Bridge Life

S usan and Tab were growing up and becoming independent. Honey and Pops had given each of the kids a car as soon as they were old enough for a driver's license. Not having to be a glorified chauffeur and having a lot of spare time on my hands, I needed a hobby. I had enjoyed bowling, but that was not an option after the trip to Colorado, where I broke my ankle. I was never very good at golf and found it difficult to find someone to play with who was as bad as yours truly.

Susan and Nell.

The obvious was right in front of me, the game I had always loved and never had time to really explore bridge.

I not only started playing bridge, but I also became involved with the organization in trying to improve our playing facilities. I was elected to serve on the board of directors and served in that position for a couple of years, and then went on to become vice president and then president.

I worked very hard to improve my game. I took lessons from everyone who was giving them locally. A woman from Ruston, Louisiana, was giving lessons in Monroe. My mother and some of her friends thought she was an excellent teacher. Her name was Jennie Bryant, and she taught at the school of Goren in Washington. I asked her if she would consider coming to Shreveport to teach, and she said if I could get enough tables to make it worthwhile for her, she would. I managed to scrape together ten tables and located a room large enough at one of the new motels in town that had just been completed. She was a grand teacher, and we would laugh and say we were playing, "Jennie says."

I was dying to play bridge with Jennie, and I wanted to prove to her how much I was improving and how good I was. I knew, on occasion, she played with my mother's friend Trudy in Monroe. I thought that for no other reason but because of my mother, she would play. How wrong I was. What I didn't realize at the time was that Trudy's husband was a druggist and supplied Jennie with her medications at no cost. I vowed to myself that she would be sorry one day.

Many years later, when I had a number of successes under my belt—both regional and national—a regional tournament was being held in Monroe, and my partner and I planned to play. My partner and I have been ranked a number one seed in all tournaments for many years. The first event we were playing in was a pair game. My partner and I were playing East/West, which meant we would be moving every round. About halfway through the game, upon arriving at the table, the people we would be playing against were so old and feeble they could hardly hold their cards. We said hello without hardly looking at them, licking our chops to collect our two tops and be on our way. We played two hands and beat them handily. As we were getting ready to leave the table, the woman said, "It was so good to see you, Nell; it's been a long time. I guess you didn't recognize me; I'm Jennie Bryant." I was speechless. As I left the table, I thought about how sad and important she had seemed at one point in my life and how insignificant she had become.

I was very fortunate to have Jim Jacoby, one of the top players in the world, as my friend and mentor. Jim and I had a mutual bridge friend who was his client. On numerous occasions, I was lucky to be the fifth person on their team and had the opportunity to play with Jim when Heidi sat out. Jim had a wonderful sense of humor. One time, when we were playing an event together, he said to me as I sat down, "Relax and have fun. This is going to be just like clubbing baby seals." I always thought the statement was somewhat funny, although a bit bizarre. After leaving the table where Jennie Bryant and her partner were seated, I finally knew exactly what he meant.

My game was shaping up, and finally, one of the teachers and top players in Shreveport, Vaughan Ellzey, asked me to play as his partner in a Board match team game. I was walking on cloud nine. I don't remember one thing about the game other than the fact that we won. Vaughn continued to mentor me, and when his regular partner decided to take up religion instead of bridge, I became Vaughn's partner of choice for many years. Vaughn was a building contractor and was unable to be gone for more than a long weekend. He only played close tournaments, mostly sectionals and a few regionals, such as Monroe, Louisiana; Jackson, Mississippi; Eldorado, Arkansas; and Nacogdoches and Longview, Texas.

I think the year was 1975 or 1976. Houston was holding their annual regional. Sandra Schultz, one of my local partners and a member of the group Vaughn was teaching, and I decided that we would give it a go in the women's pairs in the Houston Regional. Richard, Sandra's husband, would be out of town on business, and my husband, Abry, was going on a duck hunt the week of the tournament. We went to Houston, and imagine this: Sandra and I came in first at the event. Winning a regional tournament was a really big deal back in the day. The biggest perk of winning qualified us for an entry into the Blue Ribbon pairs in the next National Tournament. For the most part, only the top players in the country qualified for this event, and we were definitely in the minority. After we returned to Shreveport, the society editor from the Shreveport Times called to schedule an interview. The first question she asked was, what does this make you in the bridge world? At that time, I had only about two master points and not much knowledge of the workings of the American Contract Bridge League. The only response I could think of was that it gave me more red points than black points. Red points could only be won in regional or national-rated tournaments, while black points were awarded in club games and sectional tournaments. Fast forward to 2024, and gold points and platinum points have also been added to the list. These points are awarded only at national events.

Nothing was going to stop us; we were going to play the Blue Ribbon pairs in the next national tournament. I have very little recall of the actual event except for one round. Sandra had a very bad habit when defending a contract. This was before the rule had been passed, barring a defender from asking the declarer to see the previous trick.

As soon as a trick was played and the cards were turned face down, Sandra would say, "May I please see the last trick?" On this particular round, we were playing against a gentleman who had a metal hook for his right hand. He used this hand to turn the card over and slip it into the metal board as soon as the trick was completed. He also used the hook to dig his hand out of the board to view or play. The poor man had hardly had time to flip the cards over with his hook and shove them into the board when Sandra would say, "May I please see the last trick." The man, a perfect gentleman, always said, "Certainly." This was making me crazy. After about the fifth time she made the same request, I couldn't stand it any longer. I said to Sandra, "The next time you ask the poor guy to see the last trick, you will be playing against an empty chair because I am leaving." The man said, "Oh, Miss, don't worry, it's OK, I don't mind."

My words fell on deft ears, but somehow, we managed to finish the round.

In 1982, the nationals were held in New Orleans which was a given for me. My folks were living there, and I could stay with them. My mother and I would play in the women's pairs. I was excited. After the first three sessions, my mother and I were leading the field. My parents belonged to the Lamp Lighters Club. The club was on the 17th floor of one of the office buildings, which was not too far from the hotel the tournament was being held. The weather had turned a bit nasty, and it was raining cats and dogs. My father insisted he take me and my mother to dinner between sessions that day. I tried to beg off, knowing we needed to have a light dinner and get some rest so we could qualify. He wouldn't take no for an answer, and we were off to the Lamp Lighters Club. About halfway through the meal, the power went off. This was long before generators, and there was no way down. We missed the evening session and were out of the event.

In 1982, I was elected president of the Shreveport Bridge Association. I must admit it was a tumultuous time in my life. We were close to being in a position to finalize the plans for our clubhouse. The members were divided, and it was not a pleasant fight. The opposing members felt we could not afford to maintain a property. They proceeded full speed ahead, trying to convince the general membership. We were about to throw in the towel when five members called me one evening and asked for a private meeting. They cautioned me not to discuss it with anyone. I could not imagine what they could want other than my resignation; it looked like we were losing the battle. To my great surprise, they wanted me to know I had their full support, and they were there to volunteer to underwrite the loan for the house and property. All of a sudden, once again, it was game on. In 1983, the Bridge Association moved into their new home on East Kings Highway and Bert Kouns. Bridge was at its peak in Shreveport, Louisiana.

During this time, I was elected to serve as a representative to the Board of Governors from District 10. I attended the meetings held at the four national tournaments each year. At one of these meetings, I was appointed to serve on the National Appeals Committee. I served as Appellate Chairman for District 10 for ten years. Additionally, I served on the National Goodwill Committee and the National Charity Committee, both of which are lifetime appointments. My schedule was full while I tried to maintain top-level play.

My bridge career began to take shape; my local partner and I had qualified to represent the district in the North American Pairs at the Nationals in Hawaii. We did poorly in the event, but it was there that I met my partner of 21 years, Nancy Passell, from Dallas, Texas. Mike, Nancy's husband, approached me at the tournament and told me that he had put together an excellent women's team for the women's Knock Out that would be starting in a couple of days. Mike thought Nancy and I would make the perfect partnership, and I was thrilled. As we started to play, we began to win. We knocked out the first team we played and continued to win each day until we reached the finals. We were featured in the *Daily Bulletin*, and our team was pegged as "The Cinderella Team." Not one of us had any experience in top-level play. We weren't an embarrassment in the finals, but we were definitely out of our league. We lost to the Wei team. Betty Kennedy, one of the top women players at that time, was a member of the opposing team. Betty was also from Shreveport. Early in my bridge career, we had been friends and shared martini lunches and social bridge events. We became bridge partners and teammates, but as my game began to improve and I started coming into my own as a player, Betty couldn't take the competition and opted to no longer be my friend. She opposed everything I tried to accomplish, including the clubhouse. She dropped me as her partner and saw that I was removed from any team she was playing on. I missed my friend. Even though our team knew we were outclassed in the event, everyone considered it a major accomplishment to be second in the Life Master's (LM) Women's team. Looking back, I think I still considered it as a bitter loss.

The worm had begun to turn, and Nancy and I were in demand as a partnership for team play. Nancy and I won the LM Women's pairs and, later that year, went on to win the LM Women's Knock Out team. The win qualified us for the team trials for the world championship. The trials were in Memphis and were exhausting. In the quarter-finals, we drew the Wei team and managed to knock them out. In the finals, both teams were simply vying for position. We lost the match and went to Japan as USA 2. The press was relentless, and we were still dubbed "The Cinderella team." We knocked out USA 1 in the round robin and, after 17 days of grueling competition, went on to win the Venice Cup. Omar Sharif was on stage and presented us with the trophy. Later, he congratulated each of us during the reception in our honor. The year was 1991, and the experience was surreal.

Venice Cup Team with Legendary Actor Omar Sharif in 1991.

In previous years, winners of the world championship events had an automatic qualification for the event the next year without having to compete. About halfway through the year, the national board put out a notice that they had changed the qualifications, and everyone would have to qualify, including the reigning champions. This was quite a blow below the belt to our team. We started to throw in the towel and just say to heck with it, but we were all still performing well. So, we decided we would go for it. This year, because of the low number of teams competing, only one team would qualify. Our team led the round robin and made it to the final. The match was exactly even until the last board. At our table, Nancy and I stayed out of a slam, knowing we were off an Ace and the Queen of trumps. Nancy played the hand carefully and, against excellent defense, made her contract of five hearts. At the other table against our teammates, the opposing pair bid the slam and, after an unfortunate opening lead by our side, were able to collect twelve tricks. Our teammates came back to the table to compare, shaking their heads. Nancy called the scores for us and said, "Plus 650." Sharon, our teammate, said, "Minus 1430." It was a heartbreaker. No one said a word. There was nothing left to say; we all just scattered in separate directions, anxious to pack our bags and head for our respective homes.

Several days passed, and Nancy called. She told me she had talked to Sharon and Sue, and they were dissolving their partnership. Nancy also said she was planning to take time off because their daughter was turning thirteen, and she and Mike both felt that at least one of them needed to be at home. Bridge was Mike's profession, so it was clear where the responsibility lay. Nancy said her traveling days were over for the next few years. She wanted to be sure I had time to make other arrangements.

I didn't have much time to feel sorry for myself before my phone started ringing, but I wasn't ready to pick up the pieces and move on. The fire in my belly and the desire to compete just weren't there. Several weeks went by when I received a phone call from Becky Rogers, who had been invited to be a substitute with the partner of her choice in the team trials to be held in Hyannis Port. I told her to let me sleep on it, and I would give her an answer in the morning. Before I closed my eyes, my mind was made up, and my answer was yes. Becky called me the next morning, and before I had a chance to say anything, Becky said, "I have a problem. You are qualified because of your win, but I am not qualified." I really want you as my partner, and I only have this one opportunity to qualify. Before she had a chance to tell me what the opportunity was, I told her my answer was yes, I was up for the challenge. Bobby Wolff told Becky there was one last national, and there was a new national event, the Silver Ribbon Pairs. He thought this would be our best opportunity for either first or second place. Miracle of miracles, we came in second in the event, and the powers that be could not stop us now. We had done the impossible. We made it to Hyannis Port and managed to make it out of the round robin, which took an entire week. We played our hearts out but were eliminated in the quarter-finals. I thought we had played pretty well together. However, strangely enough, neither one of us ever made any effort to make another game.

Shortly after my return, I received a call from my friend Joanie Brook Stone; Joanie lived in La Habra Heights, California, at the time. She invited me for a visit and to play on her Knock Out teams in the tournament that was being held on the Q E 2. I had not been this excited about anything pertaining to bridge in months. Joanie had deep pockets and always hired the best players money could buy. Our teammates were Eric Rodwell and Bobby Goldman, and I was overwhelmed.

I played along for a number of years with moderate success of second and third-place finishes in national events. Most of the teams I played on were put together at the last minute with random players and no practiced partnerships.

My bridge friends in Dallas managed to have some unexpected success in qualifying for the World Championship in Bali, Indonesia, in 2001. I was honored when I was asked to captain their team. I worked very hard with the team for months to help them fine-tune their partnerships, and we were ready. Approximately two and a half weeks before our departure was the catastrophic event of 9/11. Travel into Jakarta, the capital of Indonesia, was closed. The venue for the championship was moved to an air base outside of Paris, France. We would be sequestered inside the facility for seventeen days if we made it to the finals. This was the first time I had ever been asked by my family not to go. The world was in turmoil, and no one knew what the consequences of this horrific event would entail. I resigned as captain, but not before I found what I thought would be an acceptable replacement. This was a true test of my priorities, and with no contest, my family was the winner. The team managed to finish third and swore to me that if I had been their captain, we would have won. As the story goes, this was my swan song at an international competition.

Nell, Susan, and Marilyn.

Online Bridge

While at the tournament in California, everyone was talking about the fantastic online bridge game that was going to transform the way bridge was played. I had noticed a number of stations on deck on the QE2 with signs that read "OK Bridge, Free Lessons." During free time, there were always players crowding around the computers. I had no idea how to even turn on a computer. At each station were signup sheets for those who were interested. Joanie took me around and introduced me to several of the instructors and the person in charge of promoting the program. After returning home, I contacted a few officers at the ACBL and found most were very negative about the program, saying there was no place for it in the real world of bridge. That did not faze me; I was still intrigued by the program and the ability to play bridge with someone 5,000 miles away.

Several weeks went by, and I received a phone call from one of the OKB promoters. He wanted to know if I was still interested in learning the program and helping them with the promotion. I told him I was, but I didn't own a computer, nor did I even know how to turn one on. He said he was going to be in my neck of the woods working setting up players in New Orleans, Louisiana, and Jackson, Mississippi. It would be no problem for him to swing by Shreveport and get me up and running. He told me he would send me all the particulars on which computer to order. I would need someone to set up the computer, and he would take care of the rest. I was to give him a call when the computer was ready. I wasn't sure how all of this was going to sit with Abry, but he was excited about the prospect of a home computer. Our first Dell computer arrived and was ready for use in a few weeks. I took to the program like a duck to water. Playing online was one of the most exciting things I had the pleasure of doing in years. I was given a free year's membership to OKB with the promise that I would play online X number of hours a day. I met up with players from all over the country who were also helping test the program. I actually became very good friends with two of the players from New Orleans, Shirley Lazurus and Jean Frankel. I invited them to Shreveport for the Labor Day regional. They stayed at my house, and we had a ball. We remained good friends and friendly competitors for the remainder of our lives.

For several years, we have worked hard to encourage the ACBL to partner with OKB. The ACBL's board of directors was entirely negative about Computer Bridge and explicitly told us it would never happen on their watch.

In the meantime, we kept playing bridge online, receiving no master points from ACBL, just the gratification of OKB points and performance statistics visible to members. We had our own competition, independent of the ACBL. Around 1985, the negative board of directors of the ACBL was replaced. The door finally opened to accept a new, more advanced online bridge program, BBO, that eventually became the official online ACBL bridge sight. I was teaching a number of bridge classes during that time, and I encouraged my students to join BBO and play some online. I have always said, "Bridge is my insurance against old age." I told them this was the best way to practice, learn, and prepare for something to do when they were bored and had no one to do it with.

Never in a million years did I think we would face a quarantine lasting over a year because of a disease called COVID-19. I have been amazed by the number of people I had lost contact with over the years who have reached out through letters and calls to thank me for encouraging them to pursue bridge online. The game has truly helped me maintain my sanity through difficult times in my life. I am forever grateful for being introduced to it at a very young age.

The '90s

I was at the height of my bridge career, playing thirty days of Nationals and the World Championships in 1990 and 1991. Mimi told me Pawpaw was my best cheerleader, and he actually kept files on every piece of publicity about me he could get his hands on. It was with great sorrow for all of us when he passed away in February of 1992.

I thought Mimi might return to Monroe where Aunt Ethel was, or maybe even come to Shreveport to be with us. There was no question about it; she was going nowhere and would remain in New Orleans. Buzz Harper and Les Weisinger, her dear friends and bridge partners, promised us they would never allow her to have one lonesome day and remained true to their word. Abry, the kids, and I enjoyed many years of their friendship and hospitality in New Orleans and Natchez, where they relocated after Katrina.

It wasn't too long after Pawpaw passed away that my mother received a call from Ecca's neighbor, informing her that Ecca was in the hospital in Monroe and she was unable to get there to check on her. Abry and I rose to the occasion, which opened a whole new chapter in our lives. After consulting with the doctor, it was evident she would be unable to return to her home on Island Drive and care for herself. The only logical solution to accommodate everyone was to find a facility in Shreveport so she would be close enough for either Abry or me to check on her every day.

Abry went back to Shreveport to make arrangements for a place for Ecca. I stayed in Monroe, making the arrangements to close the house. It only took one phone call for me. Nelson Able, Ecca's neighbor, had contacted me many months prior to let me know that if and when we were ready to sell the house on Island Drive, he would like first refusal.

When Abry returned, I had Ecca packed up to go. We picked her up at the St. Francis Hospital. We told her she was coming to a facility in Shreveport where they would be regulating her medication. She never returned to her home in Monroe.

Ecca's stay was during the time period of the O.J. Simpson trial for the murder of his ex-wife, Nicole Simpson, and her friend, Ronald Goldman. I was visiting her one day when one of the staff made daily rounds. She asked my aunt how everything was going. Aunt Ecca didn't miss a beat, and she said, "The food is terrible. You wouldn't feed this food to OJ, and I didn't kill anybody." Ecca said the eight years she spent in Shreveport were some of the best years of her life because she was able to see either me or Abry every day.

After Katrina and My Mother's Funeral

Freida (my mother) celebrating her 92nd birthday.

On Wednesday, August 31, 2005, my mother, Buzz Harper, Les Weisinger, Jane Coleman, and Buzz's two Chihuahuas arrived in Shreveport, safe from the hurricane. Where there is room in the heart, there is room in the home. I really can't remember how we managed, but for several days, everyone had a bed until they could figure out their next move. No one was allowed back in New Orleans.

Abry and I knew that my mother would never be able to return to New Orleans to live alone again. Convincing her of this fact was going to be a different story. Our home was reasonably large but not large enough. Slowly, we began to look for solutions as to where she would live. We made the rounds of retirement homes in the city, which, to her thinking, was unacceptable. In the meantime, my mother received an offer for her townhouse on St. Charles Avenue in New Orleans from a lawyer with cash in hand. It was four times what they had paid for it. Abry finally convinced my mother that it was the right move. She had received the best offer anyone could ever hope for.

Abry and I were frantically searching for places for my mother to rent, but nothing met her standards. One day, when I was driving down Fairfield Ave., I saw a woman placing a "For Sale" sign for one of the units at Normandy Village. I stopped the car and ran to her. I begged the woman not to sell the place before I could return with my husband. Cell phones were not a thing back then, so I ran home and called Abry. He thought the place was perfect, but convincing my mother would be a different story. She had no business experience and was pretty set in her ways, one of which was not wanting to part with her money. Abry had already decided that if my mother said no, we would buy it for her. When we arrived at the unit, my mother said, "Fairfield Avenue looks exactly like St. Charles Avenue; the only thing missing is the streetcar. Problem solved."

We called Buz Harper and Les Weisinger, who had moved to Natchez, and they immediately came to the rescue and decorated her new home to perfection. Les brought fabrics and carpet samples, and within a week, her new home looked as if she had been there for years. It was perfectly beautiful. My mother moved in and enjoyed four wonderful years. She always treated life as if it were one big party, and that is exactly what we did for the last four years of her life. When people would ask my mother how she was doing after her experience with Katrina, she would reply, "I never thought I would have to find new doctors, a new dentist, and buy new dishes at this stage in my life."

My mother passed away on her 94th birthday, February 21, 2007, at 8:00 a.m. She was returning home to Monroe, Louisiana, where she was born and raised, to be buried. We planned the funeral in Shreveport because Rose-Neath also owned Kilpatrick's Funeral Home in Monroe. The entire family went to the funeral home. While they were giving me the costs of everything, Abry went into the showroom to look at the caskets.

When it was time to select a casket, Abry had already spotted the least expensive one. There were two; one was a muck brown, and the other was a camouflage green. I was definitely not happy. I had seen a beautiful Mahogany casket lined in pale pink satin, but the price was prohibitive. Everyone seemed to think the green one was not so bad. I finally agreed and said, "OK, we will take the green one."

Arthur and Tab immediately ran for the door to get the cars. I was miserable with my decision. All I could hear was my mother saying, "Nell, how can you do this to me? You know how I hate green." I knew then that I would never have one night of peaceful sleep if I did not change the casket. The boys pulled up, and I said," Sorry, this will only take a second." I marched myself back in, found the man, and said I would like to change my mother's casket to the mahogany one lined in pink silk.

Andy Shee, whose family owned the funeral home and was a friend of ours, had been wonderful in making this painful time as easy on us as possible. The funeral home had just purchased a new limousine, which was at our disposal. The limo was large enough for the entire family. We all met at B'nai Zion, and when we saw this white stretch limo that looked two blocks long, everyone had a bit of trouble collecting themselves. As we took our seats, the colored lights on the interior were winking and blinking. The limo was outfitted with a complete bar and music. Chandler, who was 12 years old, stood there in utter disbelief with his mouth hanging open. When we hit West Monroe, we all spotted a Mexican restaurant at the same time. Everyone agreed it would be a great idea to stop for lunch. We pulled in and began to pile out of the limo, looking exactly like the Beverly Hillbillies.

As we walked into the cemetery, I heard someone say, "Oh, my God, I think someone fell into the grave!" The next thing I heard was my daughter saying, "I think it was my Dad." When I looked up, I saw two men pulling Abry out and brushing him off. Abry swore until his dying day that he did not fall; Mimi pulled him. From all outward appearances, he wasn't seriously injured, or so we thought. He entertained us with his funny remarks on the way to the reception after the funeral. My mother had a loyal caretaker, Dorothy, who was like a part of the family; she has ridden with us to her funeral. Abry said that when he hit the casket, he knew he heard my mother say, "Dorothy, answer the door. Someone is knocking." We left the reception, and on return to Shreveport, Abry said," I think I will have my foot checked out tomorrow; it really hurts." The next evening, he came home sporting a boot, as he had broken a bone in his foot.

Bill Pfeifer

It was June 12, 2012, and we were returning from a Caribbean cruise with the family. We had gone through customs and were on the bus in Ft. Lauderdale, Florida, headed for the airport and home, when I received a phone call from Jo Ann Rosenthal advising us of Bill Pfeifer's passing.

Jo Ann and Lawyer Ron Eastburn were to serve as co-executors of Bill's estate. If Abry was unable to serve, the duty fell to me. Jo Ann also notified me that Bill had left the entire contents of his home and the remainder of the contents of the shop that did not sell at the auction to Abry and me. He left the remainder of the estate, including his home and forty acres, to Sloan Kettering.

Several days later, I received another phone call from Jo Ann notifying me of a break-in at Bill's home on 779 Cafferty Road in Bucks County. She told me she had taken the liberty of packing up valuables such as silver and small items she deemed expensive at the suggestion of the police chief. The storage unit was on Highway 611 in her name, Jo Ann Rosenthal. I think the unit was named Bob's Storage. I spoke with Jo Ann several days later, and she told me she had finished cleaning out the apartment over the garage. She said, "Most of what was left was junk that did not sell at the auction."

After hearing of the break-in, I knew we had to get to Bucks County immediately. Abry had just been diagnosed with Alzheimer's, so the buck stopped with me. I called my daughter Susan, who had just finished a round of chemo at MD Anderson, and my dear, trusted friend Les Weisinger, who had dealt with antiques for many years. They both responded, "When do we leave?" My response was, "Tomorrow."

I notified Jo Ann and Ron Eastburn, the lawyer for the estate, that we would arrive at Newark airport at 3:00 pm and would like to meet with them as soon as possible. Jo Ann set up a meeting for 5:00 pm at Bill's home. Eastburn had never seen the house. Jo Ann prepared a little cocktail party, and we were all standing around in the kitchen. I had some questions, as I had never served as a co-executor before. They were both rolling their eyes at each other and at one point, Jo Ann said, "Looks as if we are all going to be in separate corners, Ron and me over here and y'all over there." I thought this was pretty strange.

I asked Jo Ann if she knew where Bill had left his jewelry. She said he did not think he had any. She mentioned that she had been in Bill's safety deposit box after he passed away, and there was nothing except a bunch of papers. I asked, "Did Eastburn go with you?" She replied, "No, I had Bill's power of attorney before his death. I was looking for the title to the car and was only there for a minute." When I spoke with Eastburn the next day, I asked him if he knew that Jo Ann had gone to the safety deposit box. He said, "No, he did not."

The next day, I asked Jo Ann if she knew what happened to the rings and gold bracelet Bill wore all the time. She said, "Oh, now that I think of it, when I went to the hospital to pick up his possessions, there was a ring with a blue stone and another little ring they had to cut off his finger. They weren't much." I told her I would really like to have them for my grandson. She said she would bring them later that day. When she arrived that afternoon, we chatted a bit. I asked her if she brought the rings. She acted upset and said, "I could not find them."

Friday, June 22

We were to meet at Ron Eastburn's office at 2:00 pm, but Jo Ann was twenty minutes late. When she finally arrived without any excuse, they both told me that, due to the inconvenience, I should have my husband appoint Eastburn as co-executor instead of me. Eastburn also said it was imperative to get an appraiser for the estate before he could release anything to me. He mentioned he knew an appraiser who would be willing to give lowball appraisals on the items we wanted and highball appraisals on others. I told him that if we needed an appraisal, I wanted someone to provide an accurate one. He responded, "My guy can pack, ship, and auction off what you don't want." I told him we had everything under control in that department. Jo Ann said, "No, you don't. You are so stressed you need to sign everything over to Eastburn and let him take care of it."

After that meeting, I realized I needed some legal help. I called my lawyer in Shreveport, who told me in no uncertain terms that he knew nothing about Pennsylvania law and knew no lawyers there. But he did know one thing: I definitely needed one.

There was a couple who were very good friends of Bill, and I contacted the husband the next day. He was the head of a very large hedge fund and had a number of lawyers on retainer. As a favor, he put me in contact with one of his lawyers. I was very impressed with this lawyer. He told me in no uncertain terms that I was the only person of the three who had anything to lose, and it would be in my best interest not to try to prove anyone was guilty of anything.

He did tell me he would have a little chat with Eastburn because there was no reason to have anything appraised. The will stated clearly that the contents of the house and cars were left to Abry and me, and the only time an appraisal was needed was when they were sold. He also told Eastburn to release them because, by law, we were at liberty to pack them up immediately and remove them. He also recommended that I relinquish co-executor status to Eastburn, which I did.

We had been in Bucks County for ten days, and I needed to get home.

Les needed to send an email, but when he tried to access Bill's computer, it was locked. I asked Jo Ann for the password to unlock the computer so Les could use it. She said she couldn't. I told her I knew she could because I had seen her using it on numerous occasions. She said, "I don't want to because Bill had awful porn on the computer." I replied, "We aren't planning on looking at the porn; we just need to send an email." She finally unlocked it.

After selecting some of the paintings and furniture Susan and Arthur wanted for their home, I booked her a flight, and she returned home to San Antonio.

Les was going to stay behind and pack up the contents to deliver everything to the right places. He couldn't do this alone, so we flew in his partner Alex and his niece to help. I stayed another week, packing up small valuables to be shipped to Shreveport, and then headed home.

It took Les, Alex, and his niece seventeen days to pack the chandeliers and fine paintings and see that the large pieces of furniture got to auction in New Orleans.

The ceilings were so tall that the chandeliers were connected to pulleys in the basement so they could be lowered to be repaired or removed. The prisms were removed and packed separately. Crates had to be built to secure the arms and base of the chandeliers. These would be shipped to New Orleans for auction as well.

Alex and Les made crates to secure the larger fine paintings and some of the smaller valuable ornaments, then loaded up Bill's handicap van. All of the contents would be delivered to me in Shreveport by Bill's neighbor in Bucks County. I planned to sell the van in Shreveport.

Most of the furniture was too massive for our homes. I personally kept most of the fine paintings, four magnificent green Murano glass horses, and a four-octave miniature piano that was made in Italy in the early 1800s. The remainder of the things that no one in the family wanted, I gave to Bill's loyal help, who had taken care of him for many years. I told them they were welcome to take what they wanted and hold a yard sale at the house with the remainder and divide the cash. Bill had made no provisions for them in his will, and I felt they deserved something for over twenty years of loyal service.

One of the things that has weighed heavily on me for years was a bequest of Bill's complete set—twelve place settings—of Royal Copenhagen China to Mary Harborg. When we opened the box, Jo Ann had marked "Royal Copenhagen," there was nothing but a bunch of grocery store Blue Willow with a lot of broken pieces. To my knowledge, the Royal Copenhagen had completely disappeared, and the set was never found.

What a learning experience; "You can't make it up!"

Missed Calling

After Abry's mishap at my mother's funeral, I realized that Abry was not as sharp as usual. I had to force myself to recognize the possibility that he was losing his memory. Abry might be losing his memory, but he never lost his sense of humor.

I told Abry from time to time that he had missed his calling. I always thought he would have been a terrific comedian. He always had a twinkle in his eyes. He was so verbally spontaneous that he almost always had the last word in any conversation. On the day we opened his "Doomsday Box," everything we needed to send him to his final resting place was in perfect order. His obit[11] even included his photo of choice. He closed his obit by saying, "If anyone says to you, nice obit, you can tell them it should be; he wrote it himself."

When Abry realized his memory was failing and that he could no longer remember to give me messages, he started calling the answering machine and leaving a message on the phone. The message he left this particular day said, "Honey, Pet Pleasers called for Button to remind him of his 10:00 am appointment." I told them, "Button could not come to the phone right now, but I would pass the message along."

---

[11] Obituary

Abry and I were still traveling a bit, and we were in Dallas, Texas, at North Park Mall. We were having lunch when the power went out. Everything being electric, the cashier who could not add two and two was unable to make change. Abry had given her a $50 bill and tried telling her the check plus tip was X amount, and that left X amount for his change. Not only was she stupid, she was also stubborn. Finally, the manager came to our aid, and after we were out of there, Abry said, "My God, that woman had a one subtract mind!"

I was Abry's chauffeur because he had not been driving for quite a while. On this particular morning, there were a lot of folks out jogging. Abry said, "Wonder where all these folks are going in such a rush in this heat?" I said, "Beats me." The next thing I hear him say is, "I guess they are trying to get there before they faint."

Several days later, I was taking Abry to the office. At the same time, we saw this really big lady in a huge motorized wheelchair holding a leash with a little toy poodle on the leash running in front of the chair. Pops said, "My goodness, hard to believe that little dog can pull that huge chair with that big lady."

Abry woke up with an earache, and I was finally able to get him an appointment that was only two days away instead of two weeks away. We arrived at 1:40 for our 1:45 appointment. We signed in and waited 45 minutes. I went to the window to find out the problem with the delay. The lady behind the desk said, "Oh, I haven't given you the paperwork yet as she handed me the paperwork." We were called at 3:30, announcing we had graduated to the back waiting room. At 4:00 pm, we were moved to a small waiting room where the nurse began interrogating Abry. I could tell he was mad as all got out.

While waiting for the doctor to arrive, Abry and I both spotted a picture hanging on the wall. The title of the picture was "Sometimes I Feel it's OK to be Me." The picture had funny little faces of children with different sayings printed under each one. One said I'm Scared; another one said I'm Concerned; others, I'm Mad, I'm Happy, Lazy,

Frustrated, and so on. Abry said, "I wonder where is the one that says 'I'm Constipated.'"

Abry now needs a restroom so the nurse shows him the way. Dr. Watkins was waiting for him when he returned and inquired how he was doing. Abry said, "Well, my plumbing is working better than my hearing." Then he said, "I am really angry because my appointment was at 1:45, and it is now 4:00 pm. Do you always run this late?"

The doctor said, "Wow, was the parking lot really full?" Abry said, "No, they had already towed off all the cars of the dead patients."

Shortly after this, we were unable to take care of Abry at home. This was the most difficult decision I have ever had to make. During this time, there weren't many facilities with Alzheimer's units. After many unsuccessful tries, we finally found a place that worked, Montclair Nursing Home. I went to see Abry once and sometimes twice a day. In the beginning, Abry enjoyed participating in the activities. One of his favorites was Bingo until one day, after a few games, he told the lady he wished they would stop giving him defective Bingo Cards. When asked about the problem, he said, "He could never Bingo."

Things were going along pretty well until we were faced with the quarantine because of COVID-19. This was awful because I was not allowed in the facility to check on Abry. My only contact with Abry was via mobile phone. One day, I asked him if he had charged his phone. He said, "No, I paid cash for it."

Abry passed away on July 18, 2020. We were still under quarantine because of COVID-19, and only immediate family was allowed at the ceremony. We said goodbye at a graveside service. Susan, Arthur, Tab, Marylyn, Chandler, Rabbi Janna, and I all returned home for a bite of lunch and to reminisce about the wonderful times we had shared with this precious man.

The Golden Years

T he Golden Years have come to pass, and the golden years can kiss my ass!

Live your life and pursue everything you want because one day, you will wake up and realize time has passed. Where did it go?

Beats the hell out of me!

L to R: Bernie, Freida, Nell, Abry, Janice, and Abry Sr.

I thought I would be young forever, capable of doing anything and everything I ever wanted. What a shock when reality struck.

Now, don't get me wrong, because I have had an exceptional life. Although, I must admit that as a creature of habit, I sometimes find change difficult to accept.

Susan, Arthur, Marilyn, Tab, Chandler, Abry Jr. and Nell.

When I was a young child, I remember my mother saying that life was a period of adjustments, and the people who handle those adjustments with the least amount of difficulty are the folks who will find the path to a happier life the quickest.

Leaving the nest and going to college was a major change, although a pleasant one. Marriage and adjusting to thinking not only of yourself but also of your partner was certainly an adjustment. Then came the responsibility of raising a family and later experiencing the empty nest syndrome when they went to college. Without even realizing it, somewhere along the way, our set of values and how we viewed life completely changed. We saw a man walk on the moon, which was a first in everyone's life. Somehow, we managed to live through the horror of 9/11, at which point I honestly believed life would never be the same. I kept asking myself what had happened to our America, "The land of the free and the home of the brave." Without really knowing how we did it, we moved on with our lives, and I, for one, began to appreciate the things I could do in a different way.

With all of the above, once again, four years ago, we were forced into one of life's major adjustments and put to the test of how to live with and survive with "COVID-19."

Abry was in the nursing home, and I was not allowed to see him. I was at home alone, with the exception of Sissy, my dog, who actually was my saving grace. I realized I had to look at each day as a new learning experience with the fear that if I didn't handle the situation well, it would mean my sanity.

When I was teaching bridge, I always tried to impress upon my students how important it was to learn how to play bridge online. For a number of years, I felt this was the direction the game was taking. Much to my delight, during the quarantine, I was in a position to fill so many hours that would have otherwise been very lonely. On occasion, when I received a thank you from a student or a friend I had encouraged to try playing online, I always had a feeling of real accomplishment.

Our lives seem to be settling down to a new normal, and I, for one, am forever grateful for my wonderful memories of days gone by.

Front L to R: Freida (my mother) and Janice (Abry's mother).

Back L to R: Marion (Abry's sister) and Me.

The Last Hurrah

January 12, 2024

It has been quite a while since I have made any entries. Life, in general, has been pretty amazing, "You can't make it up." The best part is the fabulous memories. I really thought being quarantined would be the perfect time to knock out the remainder of my book. Unfortunately, the words just did not flow.

We lost dear Abry on July 18, 2020. The entire United States was in a state of quarantine. Only the immediate family members—Susan, Arthur, Marylyn, Tab, Chandler, and myself—were at the cemetery. I tried telling myself it was a blessing that he was finally at peace. I know this sounds strange, but even though there was no quality of life in the last few remaining years of his life, there was still the comfort of knowing he was still with us. When someone says, "It was a blessing," I must tell you this, "You are never ready."

Once the quarantine was lifted, we had no problem getting "the girls" together for a game of Rummy Q and a bite to eat. Elaine, Kathryn, and Evelyn, my wonderful friends, have been a great support group through it all. The "Friday night eating and praying group," as I call them, had no problem getting back on schedule. Three years makes a big difference, though, and occasionally, some of us don't show up at the right restaurant on the right night.

Growing up, my mother always tried to impress upon me that it was very important to leave a party when you were still having a good time. With that being said, "This will be my last entry."

I've had a wonderful ride, and I wouldn't change anything about it. I love you all very much. What actually inspired me to finish this book was a quote I came across the other day, and it says:

"I am glad I did instead of I wish I had."

(Anonymous).

The End

Printed in the USA
CPSIA information can be obtained
at www.ICGtesting.com
LVHW012043021024
792718LV00017B/199